My
Facebook® *for* Seniors

THIRD EDITION

Michael Miller

800 East 96th Street,
Indianapolis, Indiana 46240 USA

My Facebook® for Seniors, Third Edition

Copyright © 2017 by Pearson Education, Inc.

ISBN-13: 978-0-7897-5792-0
ISBN-10: 0-7897-5792-3

Library of Congress Control Number: 2016946689

Printed in the United States of America

2   16

Trademarks

Warning and Disclaimer

Special Sales

For information about buying this title in bulk quantities, or for special sales opportunities (which may include electronic versions; custom cover designs; and content particular to your business, training goals, marketing focus, or branding interests), please contact our corporate sales department at corpsales@pearsoned.com or (800) 382-3419.

For government sales inquiries, please contact governmentsales@pearsoned.com.

For questions about sales outside the U.S., please contact intlcs@pearsoned.com.

Editor-in-Chief
Greg Wiegand

Senior Acquisitions Editor
Laura Norman

Marketing
Stephane Nakib

Director, AARP Books
Jodi Lipson

Development/ Copy Editor
Charlotte Kughen,
The Wordsmithery LLC

Managing Editor
Sandra Schroeder

Senior Project Editor
Lori Lyons

Indexer
Larry Sweazy

Proofreader
Paula Lowell

Technical Editor
Jerry Usbay

Editorial Assistant
Cindy Teeters

Cover Designer
Chuti Prasertsith

Compositor
Kim Scott,
Bumpy Design

Contents at a Glance

Chapter 1   Getting to Know Facebook on the Web 3

Chapter 2   Getting to Know Facebook's Mobile App 17

Chapter 3   Finding Friends on Facebook 31

Chapter 4   Personalizing Your Profile and Timeline 45

Chapter 5   Discovering What Your Friends and Family Are Up To 61

Chapter 6   Exploring What Others Are Talking About 79

Chapter 7   Updating Friends and Family on Your Activities 95

Chapter 8   What You Should—and Shouldn't Share—on Facebook 111

Chapter 9   Managing Your Privacy on Facebook 123

Chapter 10   Viewing and Sharing Photos and Videos 135

Chapter 11   Chatting in Real Time—via Text or Video 159

Chapter 12   Liking Pages from Companies and Public Figures 173

Chapter 13   Participating in Interesting Facebook Groups 181

Chapter 14   Attending Events and Celebrating Birthdays 195

Chapter 15   Playing Games 207

Chapter 16   Keeping in Touch with Your Kids and
Grandkids on Facebook 215

Chapter 17   Managing Your Facebook Account—Even When
You're Gone 227

Chapter 18   Discovering Facebook's Other Apps 249

Appendix A   Glossary 259

Index 265

Table of Contents

1 Getting to Know Facebook on the Web   **3**

Understanding Social Networking 3

Signing Up for Facebook from Your Computer 4

   Create a New Facebook Account 5

Signing In—and Out—of the Facebook Website 8

   Log On to the Facebook Site 8

   Log Out of Your Facebook Account 9

Finding Your Way Around the Facebook Website 10

   Navigate Facebook's Home Page 10

   Use the Facebook Toolbar 11

   Navigate with the Left Side Menu 12

   Use the Right Side Menu 14

2 Getting to Know Facebook's Mobile App   **17**

Using Facebook's iPhone App 17

   Navigate Facebook's iPhone App 18

Using Facebook's iPad App 22

   Navigate Facebook's iPad App 22

Using Facebook's Android App 25

   Navigate Facebook's Android App 26

3 Finding Friends on Facebook   **31**

Finding Facebook Friends 32

   Find Friends in the Facebook Mobile App 32

   Find Friends on the Facebook Website 35

   Look for Friends of Friends 39

Accepting or Declining Friend Requests 41
    Accept or Decline a Friend Request in the Facebook Mobile App 41
    Accept or Decline a Friend Request on the Facebook Website 42
    Unfriend a Friend 42

4   Personalizing Your Profile and Timeline   45

Viewing Your Timeline 45
    Access Your Timeline in the Facebook Mobile App 46
    Access Your Timeline on the Facebook Website 47
Changing the Look and Feel of Your Timeline 47
    Change Your Profile Picture from the Facebook Mobile App 47
    Change Your Profile Picture from the Facebook Website 50
    Add a Cover Image from the Facebook Mobile App 52
    Add a Cover Image on the Facebook Website 53
Editing the Contents of Your Timeline 54
    Update Your Profile Information 54
    Hide and Delete Status Updates 57
    View and Edit Your Facebook Activity 58

5   Discovering What Your Friends and Family Are Up To   61

Viewing Status Updates in the Facebook Mobile App 61
    Display the Newsfeed 62
    View a Status Update 63
    View Links to Web Pages 64
    View Photos 64
    View Videos 65
    Like an Update 66
    Comment on an Update 67
    Share an Update 67

Viewing Status Updates on the Facebook Website 68

   Display the News Feed 68

   Display Most Recent Posts 69

   View a Status Update 70

   View Links to Web Pages 71

   View Photos 71

   View Videos 72

   Like an Update 73

   Comment on an Update 74

   Share an Update 74

Personalizing Your News Feed 75

   Configure News Feed Preferences 76

6 Exploring What Others Are Talking About   79

Posts with Photos 79

Memes 83

Surveys 86

Countdown Lists 87

Links to Other Web Pages 88

Games 89

Facebook-Generated Content 90

Trending Topics 92

7 Updating Friends and Family on Your Activities   95

Updating Your Status 95

   Post a Status Update from the Facebook Mobile App 96

   Post a Status Update on the Facebook Website 97

   Post a Link to a Web Page 98

   Post a Photograph or Video 99

   Add Your Location to a Post 100

Tag a Friend in a Post 102

Tell Friends What You're Doing—or How You're Feeling 103

Determine Who Can—or Can't—See a Status Update 104

Sharing Content from Other Websites 107

Post Content from Another Site 107

8 What You Should—and Shouldn't—Share on Facebook   111

What's Good to Post on Facebook 111

Post Interesting Information 112

Post Important Information 113

What *Not* to Post on Facebook 114

Avoid Uninteresting or Unwise Posts 115

Avoid Posting Personal Information 116

Learning Facebook Etiquette 117

Carefully Compose Your Status Updates 117

Know the Shorthand 118

9 Managing Your Privacy on Facebook   123

Determining Who Sees What You Post 124

Configure Facebook's Default Privacy Settings 124

Select Who Can See (or Not See) Individual Posts 126

Limiting Contact from Other Members 128

Control Who Can Send You Friend Requests 128

Controlling Tagging 129

Restrict Who Sees Tag Suggestions in Photos That Look Like You 129

Limit Who Can See Posts You're Tagged In 131

Approve Tags People Add to Your Posts 132

Controlling Who Sees What on Your Timeline 133

Control Who Sees Specific Information 133

10   Viewing and Sharing Photos and Videos   **135**

Viewing Friends' Photos and Videos 136
  View Photos in Your News Feed 136
  View a Video in Your News Feed 137
  View a Friend's Photo Albums 140
  View All of a Friend's Videos 141
  Tag Yourself in a Friend's Photo 142
  Download a Photo 143
Sharing Your Photos and Videos with Friends 144
  Share a Photo or Video in a Status Update on the Facebook Website ... 144
  Share a Photo or Video from Your Mobile Phone 146
  Upload Photos to a New Photo Album 147
  Upload Photos to an Existing Photo Album 151
  Delete a Photo 152
  Delete a Photo Album 153
  Share a YouTube Video 154

11   Chatting in Real Time—via Text or Video   **159**

Exchanging Text Messages on the Facebook Website 159
  Send a Text Message 160
  Read a Message 161
  View All Messages 162
Mobile Messaging with the Messenger App 163
  Send and Receive Text Messages 163
  Create a Group Conversation 166
Video Chatting on Facebook 168
  Chat from the Messenger App 169
  Chat from the Facebook Website 170

12 Liking Pages from Companies and Public Figures   **173**

    Finding and Following Companies and Public Figures 173
        Search for Companies and Public Figures 174
        View and Like a Facebook Page 175
        View Page Posts in Your Pages Feed 176
    Managing the Pages You Follow 178
        View Your Favorite Pages 178
        Unlike a Page 179

13 Participating in Interesting Facebook Groups   **181**

    Finding and Joining Facebook Groups 181
        Search for Groups 182
        Browse for Groups 183
        Join a Group 185
    Participating in Facebook Groups 186
        Visit a Group Page 186
        Read and Reply to Posts 187
        Create a New Post 188
        View Group Members 189
        View Group Photos 190
        Get Notified of Group Activity 190
        Leave a Group 191
    Using Groups to Reconnect with Old Friends 192

14 Attending Events and Celebrating Birthdays   **195**

    Dealing with Invitations to Events 196
        Respond to an Event Invitation 196
        View an Event Page 197
    Scheduling a New Event 200
        Create an Event 200

Invite Friends to Your Event 202

Edit or Cancel an Event 203

Celebrating Birthdays 204

View Upcoming Birthdays 204

15 Playing Games   **207**

Discovering Facebook Games 207

Find Games on the Facebook Website 208

Play a Facebook Game 210

Managing and Deleting Facebook Games 211

16 Keeping in Touch with Your Kids and Grandkids on Facebook   **215**

Are Kids Still Using Facebook? 215

How to Connect with Younger Users on Facebook 217

Make Friends with Your Kids and Grandkids 217

Put Your Family Members in a Special Friends List 219

Share Photos and Videos 222

Chat via Text and Video 222

Play Games Together 223

Five Things *Not* to Do with Your Kids and Grandkids on Facebook 223

17 Managing Your Facebook Account—Even When You're Gone   **227**

Changing Your Account Settings 227

Access Account Settings on the Facebook Website 228

Access Account Settings in the Facebook Mobile App 229

Configure Specific Settings 229

Leaving Facebook 234

Deactivate Your Account 234

Permanently Delete Your Facebook Account 236

Dealing with Death 238

    Memorialize an Account 238

    Name a Legacy Contact 240

    Remove an Account 241

    Download Content from a Deceased Person's Account 243

18   **Discovering Facebook's Other Apps**   **249**

Using the Moments App 249

    View and Share Suggested Moments 250

    Create a New Moment 253

    Request Photos from a Friend 255

Using Facebook's Windows 10 App 255

    Navigate Facebook's Windows 10 App 256

Glossary   **259**

Index   **265**

About the Author

Michael Miller is a prolific and popular writer of more than 200 non-fiction books, known for his ability to explain complex topics to everyday readers. He writes about a variety of topics, including technology, business, and music. His best-selling books for Que include *My Windows 10 Computer for Seniors*, *My Internet for Seniors*, *My Social Media for Seniors*, *My Samsung Galaxy S7 for Seniors*, *Easy Computer Basics*, and *Computer Basics: Absolute Beginner's Guide*. Worldwide, his books have sold more than 1 million copies.

Find out more at the author's website: www.millerwriter.com

Follow the author on Twitter: molehillgroup

Dedication

To my grandkids, who make my life fun and meaningful—Collin, Alethia, Hayley, Jackson, Judah, and Lael.

Acknowledgments

Thanks to all the folks at Que who helped turned this manuscript into a book, including Laura Norman, Greg Wiegand, Charlotte Kughen, Lori Lyons, Kim Scott, and technical editor Jeri Usbay. Thanks also to the kind folks at AARP for adding even more to the project.

About AARP and AARP TEK

AARP is a nonprofit, nonpartisan organization, with a membership of nearly 38 million, that helps people turn their goals and dreams into *real possibilities*™, strengthens communities, and fights for the issues that matter most to families such as healthcare, employment and income security, retirement planning, affordable utilities, and protection from financial abuse. Learn more at aarp.org.

The AARP TEK (Technology Education & Knowledge) program aims to accelerate AARP's mission of turning dreams into *real possibilities*™ by providing step-by-step lessons in a variety of formats to accommodate different learning styles, levels of experience, and interests. Expertly guided hands-on workshops delivered in communities nationwide help instill confidence and enrich lives of the 50+ by equipping them with skills for staying connected to the people and passions in their lives. Lessons are taught on touchscreen tablets and smartphones—common tools for connection, education, entertainment, and productivity. For self-paced lessons, videos, articles, and other resources, visit aarptek.org.

Note: Most of the individuals pictured throughout this book are of the author himself, as well as friends and relatives (and sometimes pets). Some names and personal information are fictitious.

We Want to Hear from You!

As the reader of this book, you are our most important critic and commentator. We value your opinion and want to know what we're doing right, what we could do better, what areas you'd like to see us publish in, and any other words of wisdom you're willing to pass our way.

We welcome your comments. You can email or write to let us know what you did or didn't like about this book—as well as what we can do to make our books better.

Please note that we cannot help you with technical problems related to the topic of this book.

When you write, please be sure to include this book's title and author as well as your name and email address. We will carefully review your comments and share them with the author and editors who worked on the book.

Email: feedback@quepublishing.com

Mail: Que Publishing
         ATTN: Reader Feedback
         800 East 96th Street
         Indianapolis, IN 46240 USA

Reader Services

Register your copy of *My Facebook for Seniors* at quepublishing.com for convenient access to downloads, updates, and corrections as they become available. To start the registration process, go to quepublishing.com/register and log in or create an account.* Enter the product ISBN, 9780789757920, and click Submit. Once the process is complete, you will find any available bonus content under Registered Products.

*Be sure to check the box that you would like to hear from us in order to receive exclusive discounts on future editions of this product.

Lew Archer
Edit Profile

FAVORITES
News Feed
Messages
Events
Sale Groups

APPS
Live Video
Games
On This Day
FarmVille 2
Words With Friends
Candy Crush Saga
Dice with Buddies
Angry Birds Friends
Photos
Find Friends
Games Feed

FRIENDS
3M
Lakeville, Minnesot...
Burger King

Find friends

Lew   Home   Find Friends

Photo/Video   Photo Album

What's on your mind?

Friends ▾   Post

Tom French
1 min

I love this time of year!

TRENDING
Spider-Man: Artist Releases Storyboards From Canceled 4th Installment in Film Franchise
Mariah Carey: Singer Does Interview From Inside Bathtub on 'Johnny Kimmel Live'
Yellowstone National Park: Video Shows Elk Charging at Woman Trying to Take Its Picture in Park
See More

GAMES

See More

PEOPLE YOU MAY KNOW   See All
Paul Gauche
Michael Miller is a mutual friend.
Add Friend

SUGGESTED PAGES   See All

Chat

In this chapter, you find out how to create a new Facebook account and start using the Facebook website.

➔ Understanding Social Networking
➔ Signing Up for Facebook
➔ Signing In—and Signing Out
➔ Finding Your Way Around Facebook

Getting to Know Facebook on the Web

Facebook has more than one billion members online, of all ages and types. Chances are your family and friends are already using Facebook—which means it's time for you to join in, too.

About half of all members access Facebook with their desktop or notebook computers, using the Facebook website. The other half access Facebook from their mobile phones and tablets—which we'll discuss in the next chapter.

Understanding Social Networking

Facebook is a *social network*. A social network is an Internet-based service that hosts a community of users and makes it easy for those users to communicate with one another. Social networks enable users to share experiences and opinions with one another, and thus keep in touch with friends and family members, no matter where they're located.

The goal of a social network is to create a network of online "friends," and then share your activities with them via a series of message posts. These posts are short text messages, called *status updates*, which can be viewed by all your friends on the site. A status update can be text only, or it can contain photos, videos, and links to other web pages.

Your online friends read your posts, as well as posts from other friends, in a continuously updated stream. On Facebook, this stream is called the *News Feed*, and it's the one place where you can read updates from all your online friends and family; it's where you find out what's really happening.

There are many social networks on the Internet, and Facebook is the largest. (Other popular social networks include Pinterest, LinkedIn, and Twitter.) With more than one billion users worldwide, chances are many of your friends and family are already using Facebook.

Facebook was launched by Mark Zuckerberg while he was a student at Harvard in 2004. Facebook (originally called "thefacebook") was originally intended as a site where college students could socialize online. Sensing opportunity beyond the college market, Facebook opened its site to high school students in 2005, and then to all users over age 13 in 2006.

Although Facebook started as a network for college students, today it's the social network of choice for users of all ages. In fact, half of all people aged 65 or older who are online make Facebook their hub for online social activity—and browse the site for at least an hour each day.

Signing Up for Facebook from Your Computer

To use Facebook, you first need to create a personal Facebook account. A Facebook account is free and easy to create; there's no fee to join and no monthly membership fees.

Create a New Facebook Account

You can create a Facebook account from either the Facebook website or mobile app on your phone or tablet. As typing in your information from a computer is a little easier than doing so on your phone, we'll look at the website sign up here.

(1) Use Firefox, Google Chrome, Internet Explorer, Microsoft Edge, Safari, or another web browser to go to Facebook's home page at www.facebook.com.

(2) Go to the Sign Up section and enter your first name into the First Name box.

(3) Enter your last name into the Last Name box.

(4) Enter your email address or mobile phone number into the Mobile Number or Email box and then re-enter it into the next box. (Most people register with their email address, although you might want to use your mobile number if you only use Facebook on your smartphone.)

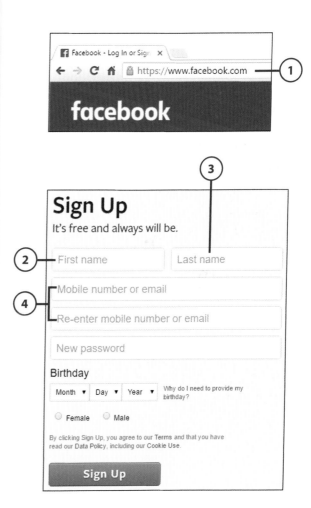

Email Address

Facebook uses your email address or phone number to confirm your identity and to contact you when necessary. You also use your email address or phone number to sign into Facebook each time you enter the site.

(5) Enter your desired password into the New Password box. Your password should be at least six characters in length—the longer the better, for security reasons.

(6) Select your date of birth from the Birthday list. (You can later choose to hide this information if you want; see Chapter 17, "Managing Your Facebook Account—Even When You're Gone," to learn how.)

Sign Up

It's free and always will be.

First name

Last name

Mobile number or email

Re-enter mobile number or email

(5) ── New password

Birthday

(6) ── Month ▼   Day ▼   Year ▼   Why do I need to provide my birthday?

○ Female   ○ Male

By clicking Sign Up, you agree to our Terms and that you have read our Data Policy, including our Cookie Use.

Sign Up

>>>Go Further
PASSWORD SECURITY

To make your password harder for hackers to guess, include a mix of alphabetic (upper- and lowercase), numeric, and special characters, such as punctuation marks. You can also make your password more secure by making it longer; an eight-character password is much harder to crack than a six-character one. Just remember, though, that the more complex you make your password, the more difficult it may be for you to remember—which means you probably need to write it down somewhere, just in case. (Just make sure wherever you write it down is kept well-hidden and secure!)

7 Check the appropriate option for your gender.

8 Click the Sign Up button.

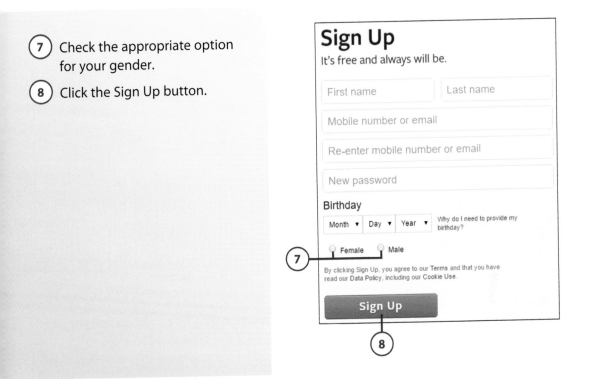

>>>Go Further

EMAIL CONFIRMATION AND MORE

After you click the Sign Up button, Facebook sends you an email or text message asking you to confirm your new Facebook account. When you receive this message, click the link to proceed.

You'll then be prompted to find friends who are already on Facebook, and to fill in a few personal details for your profile page. You can perform these tasks now or at a later time (which is probably more convenient), as we'll discuss later in this book.

Signing In—and Out—of the Facebook Website

After you've created your Facebook account, you can sign into the website and start finding new (and old) friends. You sign in at the same page you created your account—www.facebook.com.

Log On to the Facebook Site

You use your email address—and the password you created during the signup process—to log in to your Facebook account. When you're logged in, Facebook displays your home page.

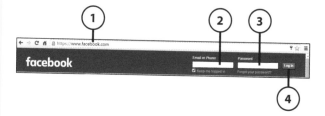

1. Use Firefox, Google Chrome, Internet Explorer, Microsoft Edge, Safari, or another web browser to go to Facebook's home page at www.facebook.com.

2. Enter your email address into the Email or Phone box.

3. Enter your password into the Password box.

4. Click the Log In button.

>>>Go Further
STAY LOGGED IN—OR NOT

If you don't want to enter your email and password every time you want to use the Facebook site, check the Keep Me Logged In option when you're signing in. This keeps your Facebook session open, even if you visit another website between Facebook pages.

You should not check the Keep Me Logged In option if you're using a public computer, such as one at the library, or if you share your computer with other users. Doing so makes it possible for other users to use your personal Facebook account, which you don't want. If you share your computer or use a public computer, don't check the Keep Me Logged In option.

Log Out of Your Facebook Account

You probably want to log out of Facebook if you're not going to be active for an extended period of time. You also want to log out if someone else in your household wants to access his or her Facebook account.

1. From any Facebook page, click the down arrow button at the far right side of the toolbar.

2. Click Log Out from the drop-down menu.

Sign Back In

After you've logged out, you need to sign back in before you can access your Facebook content again.

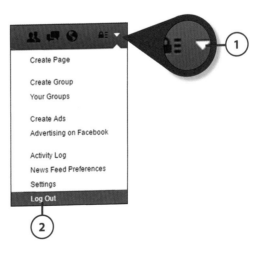

Finding Your Way Around the Facebook Website

You discover more about using Facebook throughout the balance of this book, but for now let's examine how to get around the Facebook website. When it comes to moving from place to place on Facebook's site, you have two choices. You can use either the Facebook toolbar that appears at the top of every page, or the navigation pane that's displayed on the left side of all pages. Not all options are found in both places.

Navigate Facebook's Home Page

After you sign into your Facebook account on your computer, you see Facebook's home page. This page looks a little different for each user, as it displays content personalized for you.

1. On the left side of the page is the *navigation sidebar*, or what Facebook imaginatively calls the *left side menu*. You use the options here to go to various places on the Facebook site.

2. The large column in the middle of the home page displays your *News Feed*, a stream of posts from all your Facebook friends. (It also includes posts from companies, celebrities, and groups you've followed.) At the top of this column is a box you use to post your own status updates.

3. The column on the right side of the page displays various Facebook notices and advertisements.

Use the Facebook Toolbar

The toolbar that appears at the top of every Facebook page is your primary means of navigating the Facebook site. The toolbar also provides notification when you have messages waiting or if a friend engages you in a specific activity.

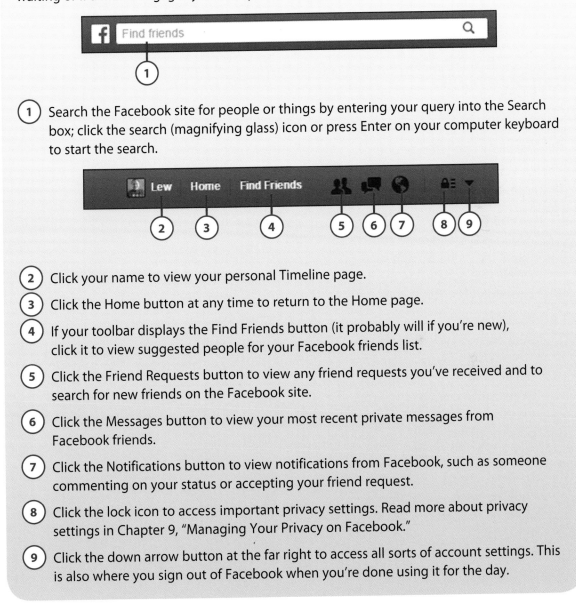

(1) Search the Facebook site for people or things by entering your query into the Search box; click the search (magnifying glass) icon or press Enter on your computer keyboard to start the search.

(2) Click your name to view your personal Timeline page.

(3) Click the Home button at any time to return to the Home page.

(4) If your toolbar displays the Find Friends button (it probably will if you're new), click it to view suggested people for your Facebook friends list.

(5) Click the Friend Requests button to view any friend requests you've received and to search for new friends on the Facebook site.

(6) Click the Messages button to view your most recent private messages from Facebook friends.

(7) Click the Notifications button to view notifications from Facebook, such as someone commenting on your status or accepting your friend request.

(8) Click the lock icon to access important privacy settings. Read more about privacy settings in Chapter 9, "Managing Your Privacy on Facebook."

(9) Click the down arrow button at the far right to access all sorts of account settings. This is also where you sign out of Facebook when you're done using it for the day.

Counting Requests and Messages

If you have pending friend requests, you see a white number in a red box on top of the Friend Requests button. (The number indicates how many requests you have.) Similarly, a white number in a red box on top of the Messages or Notifications buttons indicates how many unread messages or notifications you have.

Navigate with the Left Side Menu

You can get to even more features on Facebook when you use the navigation sidebar on the left side of the screen. Click any item to display that specific page.

(**1**) To visit your personal Timeline page, click your picture at the top of the menu. To edit your profile that appears on the timeline page, click Edit Profile.

(**2**) To read posts from your Facebook friends, click News Feed. To switch your News Feed from the default Top Stories display to instead display your friends' most recent posts, click the down arrow next to News Feed and click Most Recent.

(**3**) To view messages in your Facebook inbox, or send a private message to another user, click Messages.

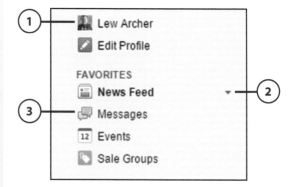

4 Any Facebook apps or games you use are listed in the Apps section. Click the name of a game or app to launch it.

5 Any Facebook interest groups you've subscribed to are listed in the Groups section. Click the name of a group to view that group's Facebook page.

6 Facebook lets you organize your friends into friends lists (not to be confused with interest groups), which are listed in the Friends section. Click the name of a friends list to view all posts from friends in that list.

7 View an upcoming event by going to the Events section and clicking that event. To view other pending events or schedule a new event, click Events.

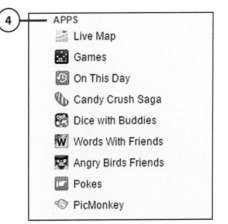

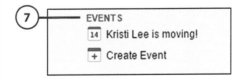

Use the Right Side Menu

The column on the right side of Facebook's Home page contains some items you might find useful, and some you might not.

1 The top of the column displays any events you've been invited to, as well as any friends who have upcoming birthdays.

2 The Trending section displays the hottest topics at this moment on Facebook. Click a topic to read posts related to that topic.

3 Beneath the Trending section is a section that sometimes displays suggested friends, and almost always a section of ads and suggested groups and pages. Ignore these as you like.

4 At the bottom-right corner of the Facebook window is the Chat bar. Click this to display a Chat list of friends who are currently online and free to chat. Click a name to initiate a chat session with that person.

Widescreen Displays

If your computer display (and browser window) is wide enough, Facebook actually displays *four* columns. The fourth column displays your games and recommended games for you, as well as the Chat list.

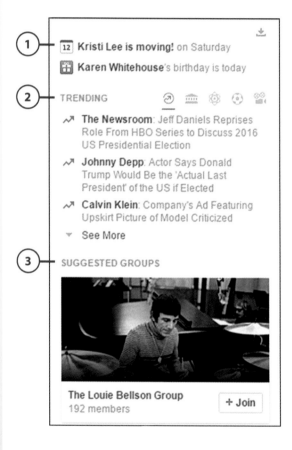

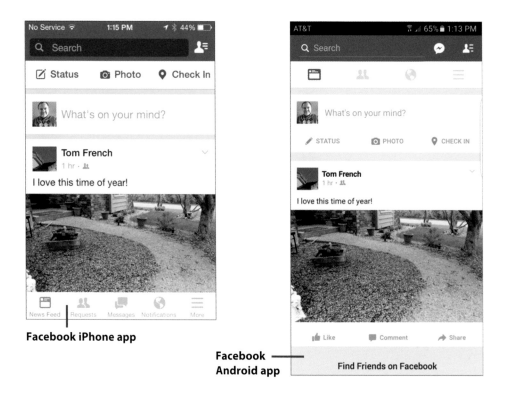

Facebook iPhone app

Facebook Android app

Facebook iPad app

In this chapter, you find out how to use
Facebook on your smartphone or tablet.

→ Using Facebook's iPhone App
→ Using Facebook's iPad App
→ Using Facebook's Android App

2

Getting to Know Facebook's Mobile App

Facebook reports that about half of its users access its service via computers, and the other half access it via smartphones and tablets. Chances are that you will check in with Facebook at least part of the time with a mobile device.

For that reason, Facebook has developed mobile apps for the iPhone, iPad, and Android devices. These apps all offer similar functionality, with slightly different layouts, so you don't have to wait until you get home to check your Facebook News Feed—or post a status update or photo!

Using Facebook's iPhone App

You can find Facebook's iPhone app in Apple's iPhone App Store. Just search the store for "Facebook" and download the app—it's free.

Logging In

The first time you launch any Facebook mobile app, you need to log into your account; tap either your name and picture or Log Into Another Account. If you don't yet have a Facebook account, enter your email address or mobile phone number, along with your password, and follow the onscreen instructions from there.

Navigate Facebook's iPhone App

When you first open Facebook's iPhone app you see the News Feed screen. This is a good starting place for all your Facebook-related activity.

1. Tap the News Feed icon at any time to display the News Feed screen.

2. Swipe up to scroll down the screen and view older posts.

3. Refresh the News Feed by pulling down the screen.

4. Tap Status to post a status update.

5. Post a photo by tapping Photo.

6. Tap Check In to "check in" (post your location only).

7. Tap the Chat icon to chat with people in your friends list.

It's Not All Good

Beware Stalkers

Using the Check In feature to broadcast your current location can alert any potential stalkers where to find you—or tell potential burglars that your house is currently empty. Because of the potential dangers, think twice about using this feature.

8 Tap the Requests icon to view and respond to friend requests.

(9) Tap the Notifications icon to view notifications from Facebook.

10 Tap the More icon to view your favorite pages and groups, as well as app settings.

Messages

All the Facebook mobile apps have a Messages icon, but it's essentially non-functional. The messaging function has been transferred to the separate Facebook Messenger app, discussed in Chapter 11, "Chatting in Real Time—via Text or Video."

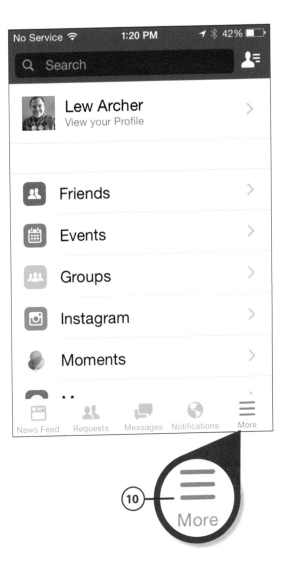

Using Facebook's iPad App

Facebook looks a little different on the bigger iPad screen than it does on the iPhone. It still does all the same things but with a slightly different layout.

Navigate Facebook's iPad App

When you first open the Facebook app, you see the News Feed screen. This screen looks different depending on how you're holding your iPad.

1 In portrait mode (held vertically), you see the normal screen with no additional sidebars. All the navigation icons are at the bottom of the screen; tap News Feed to display the News Feed.

2 In landscape mode (held horizontally), you see the News Feed on the left with a sidebar on the right side of the screen that displays upcoming events, the Chat panel (with favorite friends listed), trending topics, and more. Swipe up to scroll down the screen to view more updates in the News Feed.

3 Refresh the News Feed by pulling down the screen.

4 Tap Status to post a status update.

5 Tap Photo to post a photo.

6 Tap Check In to "check in" (post your location only).

7 Tap the Chat icon to chat with online friends.

8 Tap the down arrow in the top-right corner to access app settings.

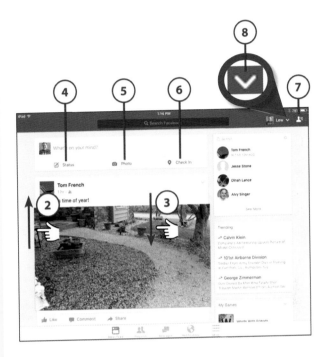

9 Tap Requests to view and respond to friend requests.

10 Tap the Notifications icon to view notifications from Facebook.

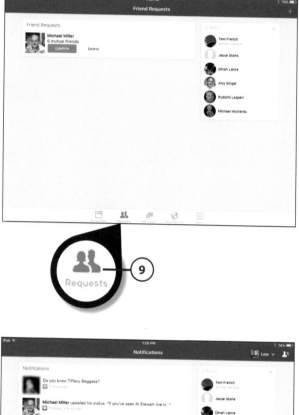

(11) Tap the More icon to view your favorite friends, pages, groups, and more.

Using Facebook's Android App

If you use an Android phone or tablet, Facebook has a mobile app for you, too. You can find Facebook's Android app in the Google Play Store; just search the store for "Facebook" and download the app—it's free.

Navigate Facebook's Android App

The Facebook app for Android looks a lot like the Facebook app for iPhone, except the navigation icons are at the top of the screen instead of the bottom.

1. Tap the News Feed icon to display the News Feed.

2. Swipe up to scroll down the screen to view more updates from your friends.

3. Refresh the News Feed by pulling down from the top of the screen and then releasing.

4. Tap Status to post a status update.

5. Tap Photo to post a photo.

6. Tap Check in to "check in" to a given location.

7. Tap the Chat icon to view friends in your Chat list.

8 Tap the Friend Requests icon or swipe right from the News Feed screen to view friend requests.

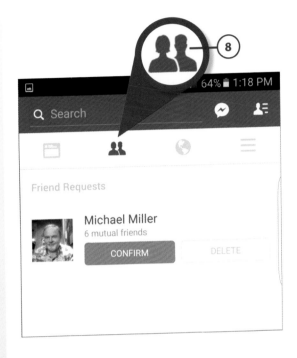

9 Tap the Notifications icon or swipe right from the previous screen to view Facebook notifications.

10 Tap the More icon or swipe right from the Notifications screen to view your favorite friends, pages, and groups, and to configure app settings.

Mobile Website

You can also access Facebook using the web browser on your phone or tablet. Just enter the URL www.facebook.com and you'll see the mobile version of Facebook's website. When you access the mobile site from your phone, it looks a lot like the mobile app; access it from your iPad and it looks more like the normal Facebook website.

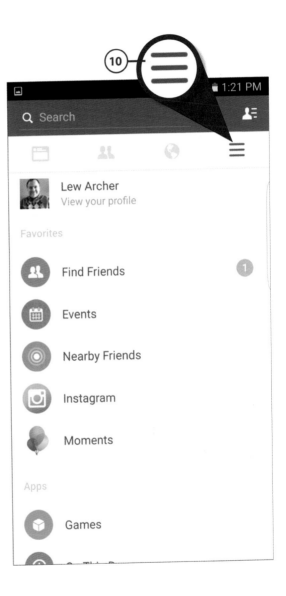

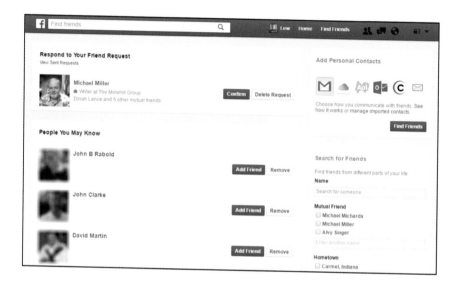

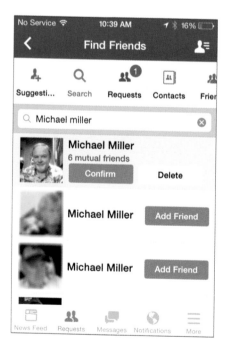

In this chapter, you find out how to find people you know on Facebook and add them to your friends list.

→ Finding Facebook Friends
→ Accepting or Declining Friend Requests

3

Finding Friends on Facebook

Facebook is all about connecting with people you know. Anyone you connect with on Facebook is called a *friend*. A Facebook friend can be a real friend, or a family member, colleague, acquaintance… you name it. When you add people to your Facebook friends list, they see everything you post—and you see everything they post.

Of course, before you can make someone your Facebook friend, you have to find that person on Facebook. That isn't always as easy as you might think, especially when you're looking for people you went to school with or worked with several decades ago. People move, women might change their names when they get married (or divorced, or remarried, or some combination of the above), and it just becomes more difficult to find people over time. It might be difficult, but if they're on Facebook, you can probably find them.

Finding Facebook Friends

Because it's in Facebook's best interests for you to have as many connections as possible, the site makes it easy for you to find potential friends. This process is made easier by the fact that Facebook already knows a lot about you, based on the information you entered when you first signed up.

Facebook automatically suggests friends based on your personal history (where you've lived, worked, or gone to school), mutual friends (friends of people you're already friends with), and Facebook users who are in your email contacts lists. You can then invite any of these people to be your friend; if they accept, they're added to your Facebook friends list.

Facebook Friends

As far as Facebook is concerned, everyone you know is a "friend"—even family members. So when we talk about Facebook friends, these could be your brothers and sisters, children or grandchildren, neighbors, people you work with, casual acquaintances, or even real friends.

Find Friends in the Facebook Mobile App

It's easy to find friends when you're using Facebook on your mobile phone or tablet. Just let Facebook make some suggestions—and then decide whether you want to accept them or not. (This example shows how it looks on Facebook's iPhone app; it works similarly on the Android version, too.)

1. Tap the Requests icon to display the Friend Requests screen.

2. Any pending friend requests are at the top of the screen. Tap Confirm to accept a request.

3. Suggested friends are displayed beneath the friend requests. Tap Add Friend to send that person a friend request.

4. Search for a specific friend by tapping the + at the top-right corner of the screen.

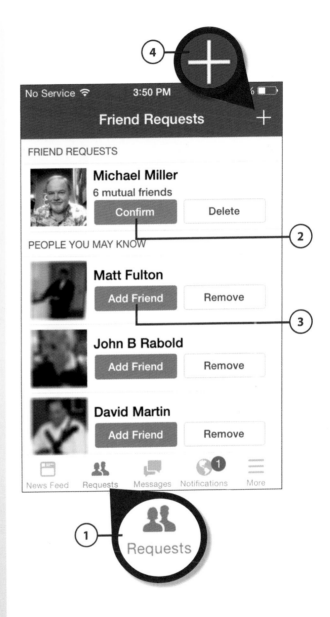

>>>Go Further

INVITATIONS

When you click the Add Friend button, Facebook doesn't automatically add that person to your friends list. Instead, that person receives an invitation to be your friend; she can accept or reject the invitation. If a person accepts your request, you become friends with that person. If a person does not accept your request, you don't become friends. (You are not notified if your friend request is declined.) In other words, you both have to agree to be friends—it's not a one-sided thing.

5 Enter the name, email address, or mobile phone number of the person you're looking for.

6 Tap Search to display matching Facebook members.

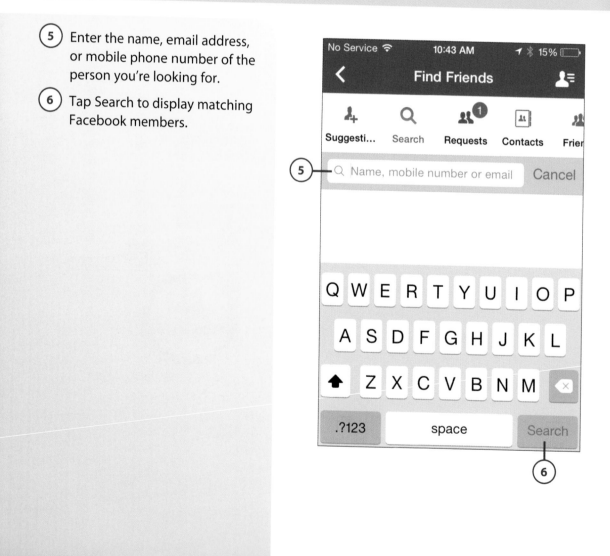

⑦ Tap Add Friend to send a friend request.

>>>Go Further

CONTACTS

Facebook can also look for members who are in your phone's contacts list. From the Find Friends screen, tap Contacts then follow the onscreen instructions to allow Facebook access to your phone's contacts. All people in your contacts list who are also on Facebook are now listed. Tap Add Friend to send a friend request.

Find Friends on the Facebook Website

The friend-finding process is similar on Facebook's website—although you have a few more options when searching for friends.

How Many Friends?

Some people like to assemble a large list of Facebook friends, to keep in touch with everyone they've known throughout their lives. Other people find a large friends list somewhat overwhelming, and prefer to keep a shorter list of close friends and family.

① On the Facebook website, click the Friend Requests button to display the drop-down menu.

② Any pending friend requests, are listed first. Click the Confirm button to accept a request, or the Delete Request button to not accept it.

③ Facebook also displays a list of suggested friends. Click the Add Friend button to send a friend request to a particular person.

④ To search for more friends, click See All at the bottom of the menu. This displays a page that lists friend suggestions and various search options. (You can also get to this page by clicking the Find Friends button on the toolbar, if you have one; it's only displayed for newer users.)

Suggested Friends

The people Facebook suggests as friends are typically people who went to the same schools you did, worked at the same companies you did, or are friends of your current friends.

---

①

Find Friends

Lew   Home   Find Friends

Friend Requests   Find Friends   Settings

Michael Miller
6 mutual friends   Confirm   Delete Request

②

People You May Know

John B Rabold   Add Friend   Remove

③

John Clarke   Add Friend   Remove

David Martin   Add Friend   Remove

Show more

See All

See All   **④**

5 In the right column of the page, scroll down until you see the Search for Friends panel. To search for someone by name, enter that person's name into the Name box.

6 To search for people who are already friends with your other Facebook friends, go to the Mutual Friend section and check the names of one or more friends. (If a particular friend isn't listed, enter his or her name into the text box first.)

7 To look for people who come from your hometown, go to the Hometown section and check your town. (If your hometown isn't listed, enter it into the text box first.)

8 To search for people who live near you now, go to the Current City section and check your city. (If your town or city isn't listed, enter it into the text box first.)

9 To search for people who went to the same high school you did, go to the High School section and check the name of your high school. (If your high school isn't listed, enter it into the text box first.)

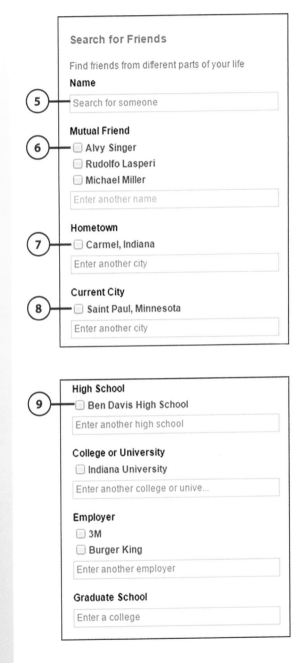

Search for Friends

Find friends from different parts of your life

Name
5 — Search for someone

Mutual Friend
6 — ☐ Alvy Singer
☐ Rudolfo Lasperi
☐ Michael Miller
Enter another name

Hometown
7 — ☐ Carmel, Indiana
Enter another city

Current City
8 — ☐ Saint Paul, Minnesota
Enter another city

High School
9 — ☐ Ben Davis High School
Enter another high school

College or University
☐ Indiana University
Enter another college or unive...

Employer
☐ 3M
☐ Burger King
Enter another employer

Graduate School
Enter a college

(10) To search for people who went to the same college or university you did, go to the College or University section and check the name of your school. (If your school isn't listed, enter its name into the text box first.)

(11) To search for people who work or worked at one of your current or former employers, go to the Employer section and check the name of that company. (If a company isn't listed, enter its name into the text box first.)

(12) To search for former classmates who went to the same graduate school you did (if, in fact, you went to graduate school), go to the Graduate School section and check the name of that school. (If your grad school isn't listed, enter its name into the text box first.)

(13) Whichever options you select, Facebook returns a list of suggested friends based on your selection. Click the Add Friend button to send a friend request to a specific person.

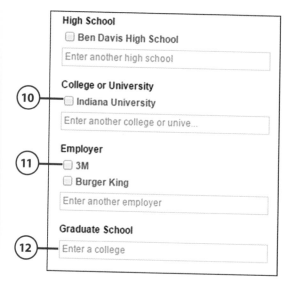

High School
☐ Ben Davis High School
Enter another high school

College or University
(10) ☐ Indiana University
Enter another college or unive...

Employer
(11) ☐ 3M
☐ Burger King
Enter another employer

Graduate School
(12) Enter a college

(13)

People You May Know

Anik Rahman Neel
University of Dhaka
+ Add Friend

Sharon Jessup
Works at UPS
+ Add Friend

>>>Go Further

FIND EMAIL CONTACTS

Another way to find Facebook friends is to let Facebook look through your email contact lists for people who are also Facebook members. You can then invite those people to be your friends.

Facebook can search contacts from a variety of web-based email and communications services, including Gmail, iCloud, AOL Mail, Outlook.com, and Yahoo! Mail.

To do this, click the Friends Request button to display the drop-down menu, and then click See All. On the top right side of the Friends page you see the Add Personal Contacts panel. Click the logo for the email service or contacts application you use, or just enter your email address and click the Find Friends button. When prompted, enter your password and then follow the onscreen instructions.

This process works by matching the email addresses in your contact lists with the email addresses users provide as their Facebook login. When Facebook finds a match, it suggests that person as a potential friend.

Look for Friends of Friends

Another way to find old friends is to look for people who are friends of your current friends. That is, when you make someone your friend on Facebook, you can browse through the list of people who are on his friends list. Chances are you'll find mutual friends on this list—people that you both know but you haven't found otherwise.

1. Click or tap your friend's name anywhere on the Facebook site, such as in a status update, to display his Timeline page.

2 Click or tap Friends under the person's name to display his Friends page, which lists all of this person's Facebook friends.

3 When you find a person you'd like to be friends with, click or tap the Add Friend button.

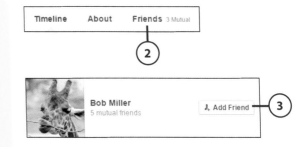

>>>Go Further
FINDING HARD-TO-FIND FRIENDS

When it comes to tracking down old friends on Facebook, sometimes a little detective work is in order. It's especially tough to find women you used to know, as names sometimes are changed along with marital status. Some women have enough forethought to enter their maiden name as their middle name on Facebook, so the Cathy Coolidge you used to know might be listed as Cathy Coolidge Smith, which means her maiden name actually shows up in a Facebook search. Others, however, don't do this—and thus become harder to find.

You can, of course, search for a partial name—searching just for "Cathy," for example. What happens next is a little interesting. Facebook returns a list of people named Cathy, of course, but puts at the top of this list people who have mutual friends in common with you. That's a nice touch, as it's likely that your old friend has already made a connection with another one of your Facebook friends.

Past that point, you can then display everyone on Facebook with that single name. But that's going to be a bit unwieldy, unless your friend has a unique name.

One approach to narrowing down the results is to filter your search results by location. For example, if you're looking for a John Smith and think he currently lives in Minnesota, use the Search Tools section at the top of the search results page to display only people named John Smith who live in Minnesota. You can also filter by school (Education) and employer (Workplace).

Beyond these tips, finding long-lost friends on Facebook is a trial-and-error process. The best advice is to keep plugging—if they're on Facebook, you'll likely find them sooner or later.

Accepting or Declining Friend Requests

Sometimes potential Facebook friends find you before you find them. When this happens, they will send you a friend request, which you can then accept or decline. You might receive a friend request via email, or you can view friend requests within Facebook.

Accept or Decline a Friend Request in the Facebook Mobile App

You don't need to access the Facebook website to see your pending friend requests. You can accept or decline friend requests directly from your mobile phone or tablet.

(1) From within the mobile app, tap Requests to display the Friend Requests page.

(2) Tap Confirm to accept a given friend request.

(3) Tap Delete to ignore the friend request.

No One Knows
When you decline a friend request, the sender is not notified by Facebook. That person doesn't know that you've declined the request, just that you haven't (yet) accepted it.

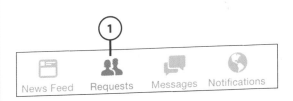

Accept or Decline a Friend Request on the Facebook Website

You can also access all your pending friend requests from the Facebook website.

(1) Click the Friend Request button on the Facebook toolbar. All pending friend requests are displayed in the drop-down menu.

(2) Click Confirm to accept a specific friend request and be added to that person's friends list.

(3) Click Delete Request to decline a given request.

Unfriend a Friend

What do you do about those friends you really don't want to be friends with anymore? Sometimes people drift apart, or you don't like that person's political views or inane posts. Whatever the reason, you don't want to read any more of that person's posts, and you want to delete him from your friends list.

Fortunately, you can at any time remove any individual from your Facebook friends list. This is called *unfriending* the person, and it happens all the time.

No One's the Wiser

When you unfriend people on Facebook, they don't know that they've been unfriended. There are no official notices sent.

① Click or tap the person's name anywhere on the Facebook site to open that person's Timeline page.

② From the mobile app, tap the Friends icon or, on the website, mouse over the Friends button.

③ Click or tap Unfriend.

Refriending

If you've unfriended someone but later want to add them back to your friends list, simply go through the add-a-friend process again.

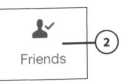

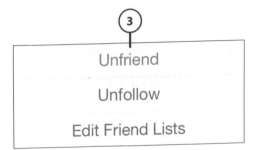

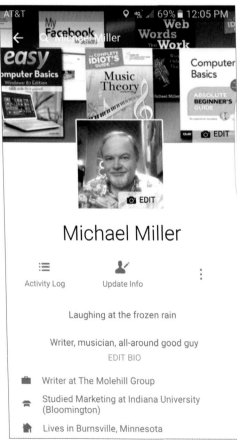

In this chapter, you find out how to personalize your Facebook Timeline page.

→ Changing the Look and Feel of Your Timeline
→ Editing the Contents of Your Timeline

Personalizing Your Profile and Timeline

When friends or family want to see what you've been up to, they turn to a single Facebook page—your personal Timeline. Your Timeline page hosts all your personal information and status updates, so that friends and family can learn all about you at a glance. Fortunately, you have some control over what gets displayed on your Timeline—it's your personal page on the Facebook site.

Viewing Your Timeline

All your personal information, including the status updates you've posted, are displayed on your Facebook Timeline page. Your Timeline is essentially your home base on Facebook, the place where all your Facebook friends can view your information and activity.

Access Your Timeline in the Facebook Mobile App

Your Timeline looks a little different in the Facebook mobile app than it does on the Facebook website. It's nothing major; the information is simply configured for the smaller size of a mobile phone screen. (This example shows how it looks on the Android app.)

(1) Tap the More button.

(2) Tap your name to open your Timeline page.

(3) Swipe up to scroll down the page and view all your information and status updates.

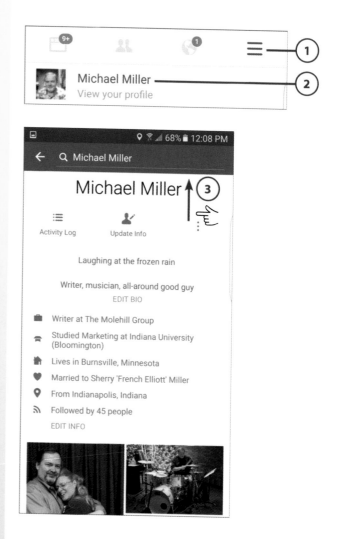

Access Your Timeline on the Facebook Website

Your Timeline page on the Facebook website is designed in a two-column format, with basic information on the left and status updates on the right.

(1) Click your name in either the Facebook toolbar or the navigation sidebar.

(2) Scroll down the page to view all your information and status updates.

(3) Click a tab to view that specific information.

Changing the Look and Feel of Your Timeline

Facebook lets you personalize your Timeline page in a few different ways. You can add a profile picture of yourself, as well as a cover image that adorns the top of the page.

Change Your Profile Picture from the Facebook Mobile App

Your Timeline page includes your account's profile picture—and this is the first thing many people change. Your profile picture is an image of your choosing (it can be a picture of you or of anything, really) that appears not only on your Timeline page but also accompanies every post you make on the Facebook site. (For example, your profile picture appears in your friends' News Feeds, alongside each of your status updates.)

You can easily change the image that appears as your profile picture. Some users change this image frequently; others find a photo they like and stick to it.

(1) Open your Timeline page and tap your profile picture. (If you don't yet have a picture, tap the generic icon that's there, instead.)

(2) Tap Upload Video or Photo (Android) or Select Profile Picture (iOS) to display pictures on your phone.

(3) Select an existing photo by navigating to and tapping the photo you want to use and then skip to step 7, or...

(4) Take a new photo with your phone's camera by tapping the Camera tile or icon.

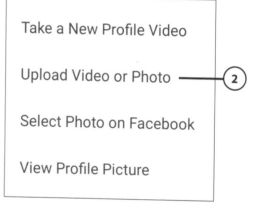

5 Tap to select the rear-facing (selfie) camera.

6 Smile and then tap to take a picture of yourself. If prompted, tap OK to accept the photo.

7 Pinch or stretch to zoom out of or into the photo.

8 Tap Use to use this photo. Your profile picture is now changed.

Change Your Profile Picture from the Facebook Website

You can just as easily choose a picture stored on your computer to use as your profile picture.

(1) Open your Timeline page, mouse over your profile picture, and click Update Profile Picture to display the Update Profile Picture panel. (If you don't yet have a picture, click the generic icon that's there, instead.)

(2) Click one of the suggested photos, if it's one you want to use and then skip to step 6, or…

(3) Choose another photo on your computer by clicking Upload Photo to display the Choose File to Upload or Open dialog box. (Skip to step 9 if you instead want to take a photo with your webcam.)

(4) Navigate to and select the photo you want to use.

(5) Click the Open button.

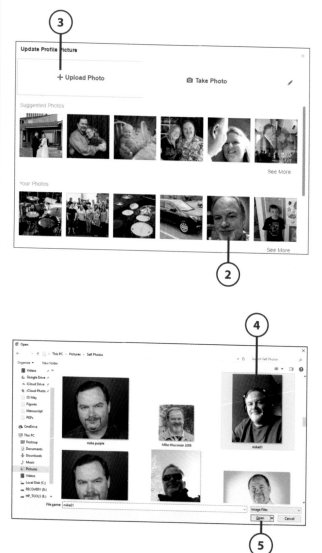

6. Use the slider to zoom into or out of the photo—or skip to step 8 if you're happy with the picture as-is.

7. Drag the photo to reposition the contents.

8. Click Crop and Save to make this your profile picture.

9. You can also shoot a new profile picture using your computer's webcam. From the Update Profile Picture pane, click Take Photo to display the Take Photo panel.

10. Smile and click the Take Photo button; this initiates a 3-2-1 countdown before the picture is taken.

11. If you like the photo, click Save. If not, click Retake Photo.

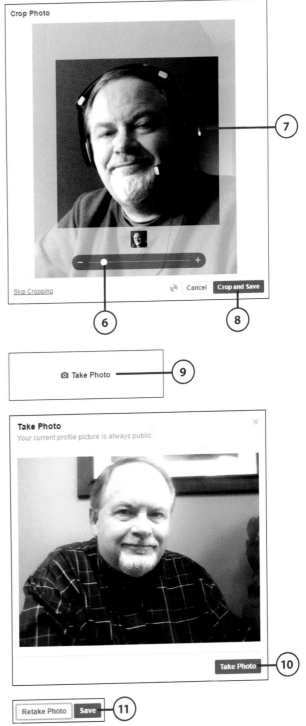

Add a Cover Image from the Facebook Mobile App

By default, your profile picture appears against a shaded background at the top of your Timeline page—not very visually interesting. You can, however, select a background image (called a *cover image*) to appear on the top of the page. Many people choose landscapes or other artistic images that provide an interesting but non-obtrusive background to their profile picture; others choose more personal photos as their covers.

1. Tap the existing cover image or, if you haven't yet added an image, the Edit or Add Cover Photo button.

2. Tap Upload Photo. (Or, if you want to select from a photo you've previously uploaded, tap Select Photo on Facebook.)

3. Navigate to and tap the photo you want to use.

4. The photo is now previewed on your Timeline page. Drag the photo to reposition it, if necessary.

5. Tap Save.

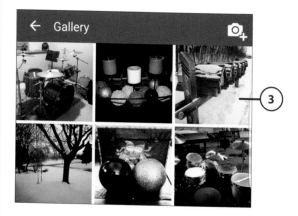

Cover Image Specs

Your cover image should be wider than it is tall. The ideal size is 851 pixels wide by 315 pixels tall—although if you upload a smaller or larger image, Facebook resizes it to fill the space.

Add a Cover Image on the Facebook Website

It's just as easy to use a photo from your computer as the cover image, using the Facebook website.

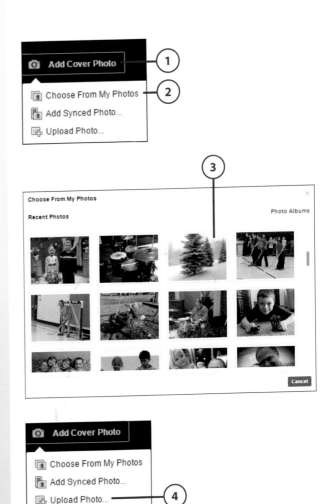

1. Mouse over the top-left corner of the existing cover photo or generic image and click the Update Cover Photo or Add Cover Photo button. A pop-up menu with several options displays.

2. Select from a photo already uploaded to Facebook by clicking Choose from My Photos to display the Choose from My Photos panel.

3. Click one of the photos you see, or click Photo Albums to select a photo from one of your photo albums.

4. Select a photo stored on your computer by clicking the Upload Photo option.

5 Navigate to and select the picture you want to use.

6 Click the Open button.

7 You're prompted to reposition the cover image by dragging it around the cover image space. Use your mouse to reposition the image as necessary.

8 Click the Save Changes button.

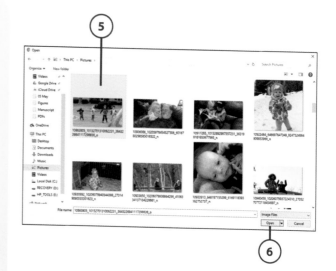

Reposition Your Cover Image

You can reposition the picture used as your cover image at any time. Mouse over your cover image, click Update Cover Photo, and then click Reposition. Use your mouse to position the image as you wish, and then click the Save Changes button.

Editing the Contents of Your Timeline

You can edit most of the personal information displayed on your Timeline page, to either add new events or hide information you'd rather not leave public. You can also choose to hide unwanted status updates.

Update Your Profile Information

Many people don't fully complete their profiles when first joining Facebook. Maybe you forgot to include certain information, or maybe you entered it wrong. In any case, Facebook lets you easily edit or update the personal information in your Facebook profile. You can also select who can view what information.

The process of changing your profile info is similar whether you're using the Facebook mobile app or website.

>>>*Go Further*

THE MORE FACEBOOK KNOWS...

All the personal information that Facebook requests of you is optional—you don't have to enter it if you don't want to. For security reasons, you might share less. On the other hand, the more Facebook knows about you, the better it can suggest appropriate activities and match you with potential friends. For example, Facebook makes more and more relevant friend suggestions when you add every school you've attended and every employer you've worked for. So enter as much information as you're comfortable with, and let it go at that.

(1) Go to your Timeline page and click or tap Update Info.

(2) This displays a special page for entering and editing your information. In the Facebook mobile app, swipe to get to the section you want to edit. On the Facebook website, click the type of info you want to edit on the left and then scroll down to a specific section.

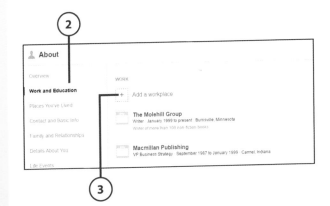

(3) Click or tap any item you want to add, such as Add a Workplace or Add Education.

4 You see a series of fields you can fill in for specific information. Enter the information as requested.

5 Click or tap the Privacy button for this item, and then select who can view this information—Public, Friends, Only Me, or Custom.

Only Me

Selecting the Only Me option makes that piece of information visible only to yourself. No one else on Facebook, not even your friends, can see it.

6 Click Save Changes or tap Save to close editing on this item. Repeat these steps as necessary to add more information.

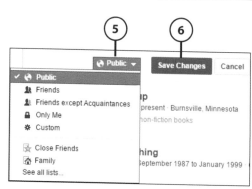

>>>Go Further
WHO KNOWS WHAT?

Not everyone viewing your profile needs to see all your information. For example, you might want everyone to view your birthdate, but not necessarily the year of your birth. You might want only your friends to view your relationship status, or you might not want to share your personal contact information with anyone. You can fine-tune your profile as granularly as you like, in this fashion, to create a clear division between your public and private lives.

Hide and Delete Status Updates

In addition to your personal information, your Timeline displays all the status updates you've made on Facebook, from the first day you signed up to just now. You don't have to display every single status update, however; if there's an embarrassing update out there, you can choose to either hide it from view or completely delete it.

1. Go to your Timeline page, scroll to a specific status update, and click or tap the down arrow in the top-right corner to display a menu of options.

2. Click or tap Hide from Timeline to hide this update but not permanently delete it. (Hidden posts can be unhidden in the future.)

3. Click Delete to permanently delete this update from Facebook. (Deleted posts cannot be undeleted.)

Not Everything Can Be Deleted

Not all status updates can be deleted. If the Delete option doesn't appear, you should opt to hide the update instead.

View and Edit Your Facebook Activity

Your Timeline page presents all your Facebook activity in a nice, visually attractive fashion. However, if you want a more straightforward view of what you've done online, you can display and edit your Activity Log. This is a chronological list of everything you've done on the Facebook site, from status updates to links to comments you've made on others' posts.

>>>*Go Further*

CLEAN UP YOUR TIMELINE

Many users find the Activity Log the most efficient way to clean up entries on their Timelines. It's easier to see what's posted (and available to post) from the more condensed Activity Log listing than it is by scrolling through the entire Timeline.

(1) From your Timeline page, click View Activity Log (on the website) or tap Activity Log (in the mobile app). This displays your Facebook Activity Log.

(2) In the mobile app, tap the down arrow for a post and then tap either Hide from Timeline, Allow on Timeline (to unhide a previously hidden post), or Delete.

(3) On the Facebook website, click the Allowed on Timeline (pencil) button for an item, and then check Hidden from Timeline to hide that item from your Timeline. (To unhide a previously hidden item, check Allowed on Timeline.)

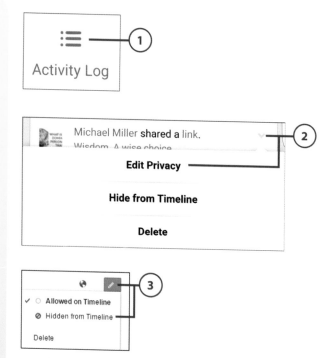

4 Change who can view an item by clicking the Privacy button and selecting Public, Friends, Only Me, or Custom. (In the mobile app, tap the down arrow then tap Edit Privacy.)

✓ Public	
Friends	
Friends except Acquaintances	
Only Me	
Custom	
Close Friends	
Family	
See all lists...	

→ Viewing Status Updates in the News Feed in the Facebook Mobile App
→ Viewing Status Updates on the Facebook Website
→ Personalizing Your News Feed

Discovering What Your Friends and Family Are Up To

After you've added someone to your Facebook friends list, you'll be kept up to date on what that person is doing and thinking. Everything that person posts to Facebook—text updates, photos, videos, you name it—automatically appears in your News Feed.

Viewing Status Updates in the Facebook Mobile App

Facebook's News Feed is where you keep abreast of what all your friends are up to. When a person posts a status update to Facebook, it appears in your personal News Feed. (We're using the Android app for the examples in this chapter; the iPhone app works similarly.)

Display the Newsfeed

The News Feed is front and center in the Facebook's mobile app; it's the default view when you open the app on your phone or tablet.

(1) Tap the News Feed icon to display the News Feed.

(2) Swipe up to scroll down the page and view more updates.

(3) Pull down the screen to refresh the News Feed.

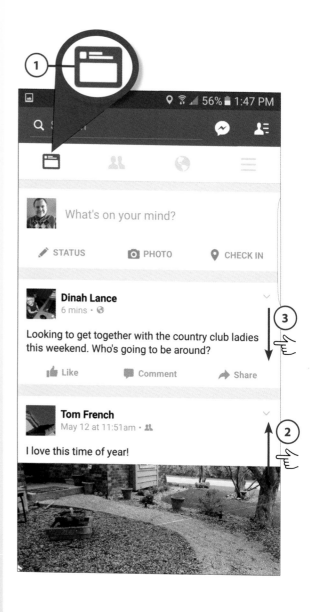

View a Status Update

The News Feed consists of status updates made by your friends and by company and celebrity pages you've liked on Facebook. It also includes posts from Facebook groups you've joined, as well as the occasional advertisement.

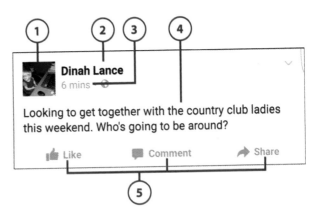

(1) The poster's profile picture appears in the top-left corner.

(2) The poster's name appears at the top of the post, beside the profile picture. To view the poster's Timeline page, tap the person's name.

(3) When the item was posted (how many minutes or hours or days ago) is displayed beneath the poster's name.

(4) The content of the status update appears under the top portion of the post. This can include text, images, or a video.

(5) Links to like, comment on, and share this post appear after the post content.

View Links to Web Pages

Many status updates include links to interesting web pages. You can tap a link to view the web page posted by your friend.

1 The title of the linked-to web page appears under the normal status update text. (Many links also included images from the linked-to page, as well as short descriptions of the pages' contents.) Tap the title or image to display the linked-to web page in a screen in the Facebook app.

2 Tap the X (Android) or back arrow (iOS) to return to the News Feed.

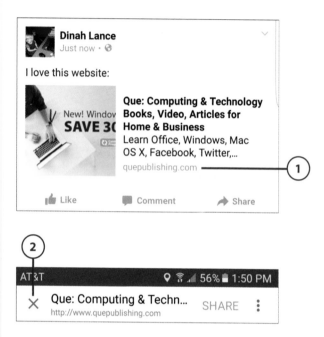

View Photos

Many Facebook users post photos in addition to or instead of text messages. You can view these photos in the News Feed itself, or tap the photos to view them larger on your mobile device.

1 Tap a picture to view it on its own screen.

② Tap Like to like this photo.

③ Tap Comment to leave a comment on this photo.

④ Tap Share to share this photo with your Facebook friends.

⑤ Tap the More (three dot) button and then tap Save Photo to download this photo to your phone or tablet.

View Videos

Facebook users can also post videos with their status updates. These can be videos uploaded from their phones or videos uploaded to YouTube.

① A thumbnail image from the video appears in the body of the status update, with a "play" arrow superimposed on top of the image. Depending on how you've configured your Facebook settings, the video may start playing automatically when the post is viewed. If it doesn't, tap the image to play the video.

Video Settings

Learn how to adjust the automatic video playback setting in Chapter 17, "Managing Your Facebook Account— Even When You're Gone."

(2) To pause playback, tap the video and then tap the Pause button.

(3) To view the video full screen, tap the full screen button.

Like an Update

Facebook offers several ways to "like" your favorite posts. You can give a post a simple "thumbs up" or apply other emojis to express your feelings.

Emojis

An emoji is a small digital image or icon used to express an emotion, idea, or opinion.

(1) To "like" a post, tap the Like icon.

(2) To view who else has liked this post, tap the Like icon.

(3) To express a different emotion, tap and hold the Like icon to display a variety of emojis.

(4) Tap the emoji you want to apply.

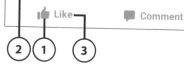

Comment on an Update

Want to share your opinions about a given status update? You can.

1. View others' Comments by tapping the comments indicator.

2. Leave your own comment by tapping the Comment icon to display the Write a Comment screen.

3. Use your device's onscreen keyboard to enter your thoughts into the Write a Comment Box.

4. Tap Post or the Send icon to post your comments.

Dinah Lance
48 mins · 🌐

Looking to get together with the country club ladies this weekend. Who's going to be around?

👍 You and 1 other   1 Comment ─── ①

👍 Like   💬 Comment   ➤ Share

②

👍 **You and Michael Miller**   ❯

Michael Miller
Sherry says she'll be there!

Just now · Like · Reply

📷 You bet

➤

③   ④

Share an Update

You can also share status updates in your News Feed with your other Facebook friends.

1. Tap the Share icon.

Dinah Lance
48 mins · 🌐

Looking to get together with the country club ladies this weekend. Who's going to be around?

👍 You and 1 other   1 Comment

👍 Like   💬 Comment   ➤ Share

①

(2) When prompted, tap Share Now (iOS) or Share Post Now (Android) to share the post as-is, without any additional comments.

(3) To add your comments to the post, tap Write Post.

(4) Use your device's onscreen keyboard to add your text comments.

(5) Tap Post to repost the update to your friends.

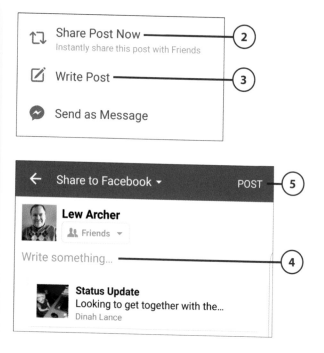

Viewing Status Updates on the Facebook Website

The News Feed and status updates work pretty much the same way on the Facebook website as they do in the mobile app. In fact, you have a few more options available when you access Facebook from your notebook or desktop computer.

Display the News Feed

You can easily get to the News Feed from anywhere on the Facebook site, using the ever-present toolbar at the top of every Facebook page.

1. From the Facebook toolbar, click the Home button.

2. The News Feed displays in the center of the page. Note that in the navigation sidebar (left-side menu), the top item, News Feed, is selected. If you later choose to display other content (by clicking an item in the sidebar), you can return to the News Feed by clicking News Feed in the sidebar.

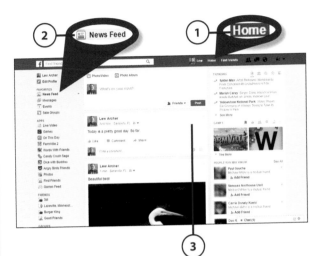

3. The News Feed lists what Facebook deems to be your most relevant or interesting posts at the top. Scroll down to view additional posts.

Display Most Recent Posts

By default, your News Feed displays what Facebook calls your Top Stories. These may not actually be the items you're most interested in, or even the most recent posts from your friends. One of the benefits of using Facebook's website (in contrast to using the mobile app) is that you can change the News Feed to display your friends' most recent posts.

1. To display the most recent posts, move to the navigation sidebar, click the down arrow next to the News Feed item, and then click Most Recent.

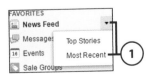

(2) To redisplay the most important posts, click the down arrow next to the News Feed item in the sidebar, and then click Top Stories.

View a Status Update

Each status update in your News Feed consists of several distinct components.

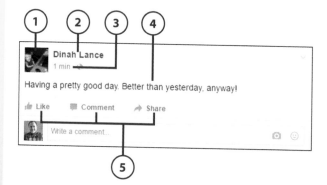

(1) The poster's profile picture appears in the top-left corner.

(2) The poster's name appears at the top of the post, beside the profile picture. To view more information about this person, mouse over his or her name; to view the poster's Timeline page, click the person's name.

(3) When the item was posted (how many minutes or hours or days ago) is displayed beneath the poster's name.

(4) The content of the status update appears under the top portion of the post. This can include text, images, or a video.

(5) Links to like, comment on, and share this post appear after the post content.

View Links to Web Pages

Many status updates include links to interesting web pages. You can click a link to view the web page posted by your friend.

(1) The title of the linked-to web page appears under the normal status update text. Click the title to display the linked-to web page in a new tab of your web browser.

(2) Many links include images from the linked-to page, as well as a short description of the page's content. (You can also click the image to go to the linked-to page.)

View Photos

It's common for Facebook users to post photos of various types. These photos appear as part of the status update.

(1) The photo appears in the body of the status update. (If more than one photo is posted, they may appear in a tiled collage or in side-scrolling display.) To view a larger version of any picture, click the photo in the post.

(2) This displays the photo within its own *lightbox*—a special window superimposed over the News Feed. To close the photo lightbox, click the X in the upper-right corner.

View Videos

Many Facebook users post their own home movies so their friends can view them.

(1) A thumbnail image from the video appears in the body of the status update. Some videos start playing automatically when the post is viewed. Others appear with a "play" arrow superimposed on top of the image; click the image to play the video.

(2) If the video plays with the sound muted, mouse over the video to display the playback controls and then click the Volume (speaker) button and adjust the volume.

(3) Pause playback by mousing over the video and then clicking the Pause button.

(4) View the video full screen by clicking the full screen button.

Like an Update

When you "like" a friend's status update, you give it a virtual "thumbs up." It's like voting on a post; when you view a status update, you see the number of "likes" that post has received.

(**1**) Click the Like icon to view others who have liked this post.

(**2**) To add a simple "like," click Like underneath the status update.

(**3**) To express another emotion, mouse over the Like icon to view a selection of emojis.

(**4**) Click the emoji you want to use.

Dislike and Unlike

While there is no corresponding "dislike" feature on Facebook, there is an Angry emoji that you can apply. You can also "unlike" any post you've previously liked; just click the colored Like icon to change your opinion.

Comment on an Update

Sometimes you want to comment on a given post, to share your thoughts about the post with your friend. You do this by leaving a public comment, which can then be seen by others viewing the original post.

(1) Although you can click the Comment link below the post, in most cases that isn't necessary. (You only need to click Comment if the Write a Comment box is not visible beneath the post.)

(2) Type your comment into the Write a Comment box and press Enter.

(3) Comments made by other users appear underneath the original post.

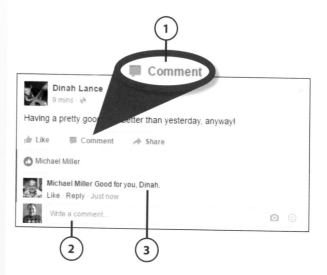

Share an Update

Occasionally, you'll find a status update that is interesting or intriguing enough you want to share it with all of your friends. You do this via Facebook's Share feature.

(1) Click Share underneath the original post to display a variety of sharing options.

(2) Click Share to display the Sharing panel.

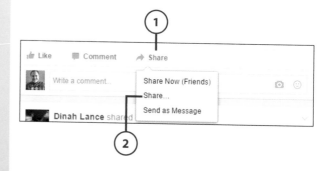

3 Enter any comments you might have on this post into the Say Something About This area.

4 Click the Post button.

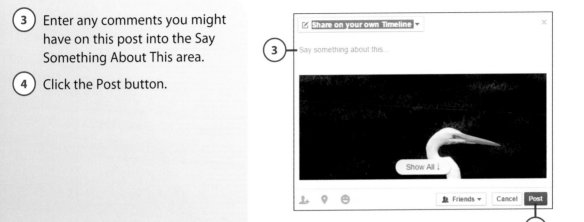

>>>Go Further

SHARE PRIVATELY

If you'd rather share a post privately with selected friends, click Share and then select Send as Message. When the Share in a Private Message dialog box appears, enter the friends' names into the To section, write a short message, and then click the Send button.

Personalizing Your News Feed

Facebook tries to pick those status updates that are most important to you. The operative word here is "tries;" Facebook's various analyses and algorithms sometimes get it right, but just as often feed you updates in which you have little interest, while at the same time hiding updates that might be important to you.

Fortunately, Facebook lets you manually fine-tune the items that appear in your News Feed. You can do this from either the mobile app or Facebook website; the settings you set in one place apply to all the devices you use to read your News Feed.

Configure News Feed Preferences

You can personalize your News Feed by prioritizing whose posts you see first; unfollowing people whose posts you don't want to see; and reconnecting with people you previously unfollowed. The Facebook website even lets you discover Pages from companies and celebrities in which you might be interested.

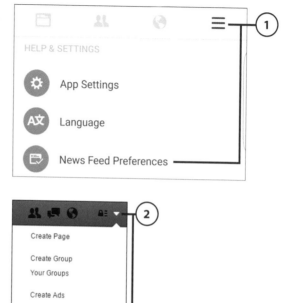

(1) In the Android mobile app, tap the More icon and then scroll down and tap News Feed Preferences. In the iPhone app, tap More, tap Settings, and then tap News Feed Preferences.

(2) On the Facebook website, click the down arrow in the toolbar and then click News Feed Preferences.

(3) Put your favorite users at the top of the News Feed by clicking or tapping Prioritize Who You See First and then clicking or tapping those users.

4 Remove unwanted users from your News Feed by clicking or tapping Unfollow People to Hide Their Posts and then clicking or tapping those users you don't want to see.

5 Restore unfollowed users to your News Feed by clicking or tapping Reconnect with People You Unfollowed and then clicking or tapping the given user.

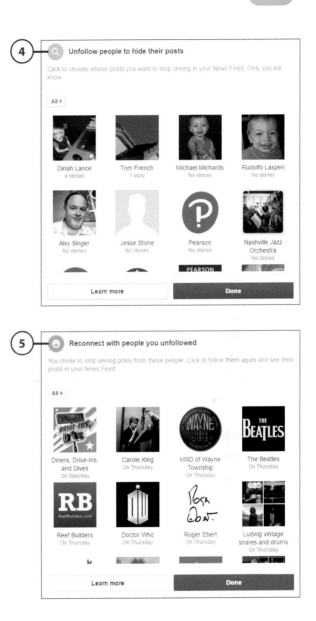

Lew Archer
Just now · Lakeville, MN · 👥

A fun selfie with the grandkids.

👍 Like 　　💬 Comment 　　↗ Share

Write a comment...　　　　　　　　　　　📷 ☺

Press Enter to post.

In this chapter, you discover what types of posts are the most popular among Facebook users.

→ Posts with Photos
→ Memes
→ Surveys
→ Countdown Lists
→ Links to Other Web Pages
→ Games
→ Facebook-Generated Content
→ Trending Topics

Exploring What Others Are Talking About

Everything goes in cycles—including Facebook posts. What was popular last year isn't so popular today.

The posts you're most likely to see in your News Feed reflect what other Facebook users like to see. Facebook uses a proprietary algorithm to determine what the "top stories" are in your Top Stories feed, but in general it's those types of posts that other users are most apt to like, share, or comment on.

What, then, is most likely to show up in your News Feed? It's all about things you can view at a glance.

Posts with Photos

Facebook started out as pretty much a text-only service; that is, you posted status updates that told your story in words, not pictures.

That's changed. Facebook, like other old and new media, has become more visual. This is due to the simple fact that most people prefer looking at pictures to reading text. We are a visual society, and Facebook reflects this.

In reality, this means that more people look at a post that contains a photo than one that's just text. You can still include that same text in a photo post, of course, but it's the picture that gets people's attention.

If you post that text *without* an accompanying photo, fewer friends look at it, and it's less likely that they'll even see it. That's because Facebook aims to show you posts that you and other users are more likely to interact with, and fewer people click Like or Comment or Share for text-only posts. Because fewer people interact with text-only posts, Facebook shows fewer of them in your News Feed.

So if you want your friends to see more of your posts, you need to post pictures in addition to your text. It certainly helps if the picture has something to do with what you're posting, and the more appealing the picture, the more eyeballs you'll attract. But the key thing is to get some sort of visual in as many posts as possible.

And that is why so many posts from your friends include pictures—all types of pictures.

(1) Many photos posted to Face-book are of the poster doing something interesting. Friends always like to see what you're up to.

(2) Other photos are of things like the poster at an interesting location. Friends like to see where you've been.

(3) Some people post pictures of a location—such as a night out on the town or a special vacation spot. Sometimes a good location photo is even more appealing than a picture with someone in it.

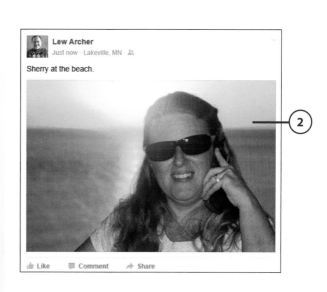

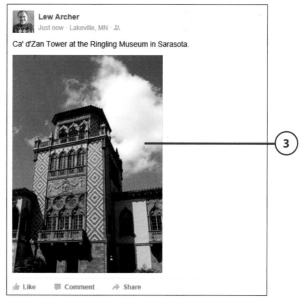

(4) Lots of Facebookers post
selfies—pictures the poster
takes of himself, typically with a
smartphone camera. Selfies can
accompany any kind of post—
even if someone's just ranting
about life in general.

(5) Of course, you'll see lots of
people posting pictures of other
people they're with—especially
their kids and grandkids. Most
people love to see cute pictures
of young kids.

Lew Archer
Just now · Lakeville, MN · 👥

Did I mention that it's cold in Minnesota?

👍 Like   💬 Comment   ➤ Share

4

Lew Archer
Just now · Lakeville, MN · 👥

Lael and Judah digging in the dirt.

👍 Like   💬 Comment   ➤ Share

5

(6) Then there are those pictures that people post of their pets. Some (but certainly not all) people like to see cute pet pictures. (But not too many of them, please!)

Lew Archer
Just now · Lakeville, MN ·

Kaylee likes to play in the snow.

Like   Comment   Share

Pictures for the Sake of Pictures

I know some Facebook users who simply attach random or mostly irrelevant photos to their posts, knowing that this alone will help them get placed in more of their friends' News Feeds. But it's better if the images you use have something to do with what you're posting about.

Memes

A lot of what you see on Facebook are posts that others have seen in their News Feeds, and then shared with their friends. When a post gets shared and shared and shared again, it becomes *viral*—that is, it spreads quickly from person-to-person, kind of like a virus does in the real world. Viral posts on Facebook, however, aren't dangerous. Mostly, they're fun.

The most popular viral posts get repeated so often that they become *memes*. A meme is a concept or catchphrase or image that spreads in a viral fashion over the Internet. Some memes are repeated exactly, but most are adaptable in different ways.

While memes are essentially passing fads, they do get a lot of likes and shares, which boosts their popularity on Facebook. Chances are a meme you see in your News Feed today (and tomorrow and the next day) will wear out its welcome in a few weeks.

(1) Most Facebook memes are pictures of something familiar or someone famous, with humorous text superimposed on the image. You may see multiple instances of that same meme, with different humorous text on the same picture.

(2) Many memes use pictures of cute or ugly animals to humorous effect.

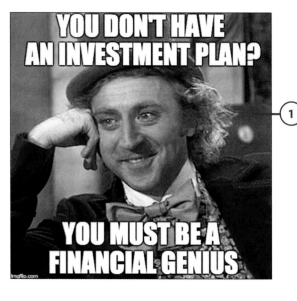

(3) Some memes, like the "what people think I do" meme, use multiple pictures to get the point across.

(4) Some memes are just funny sayings accompanied by a generic or ironic illustration, kind of like a funny greeting card.

Real Estate Developers

What my friends think I do   What my mom thinks I do   What society thinks I do

What architects think I do   What I think I do   What I really do

(3)

My favorite springtime fashion accessories are antihistamines.

someecards

(4)

Surveys

A specific type of meme that has become increasingly popular of late is the survey. This typically consists of a picture that boasts the results of someone taking the survey; you're prompted to click the picture or link to take the survey yourself.

Most of these surveys are fun and not very scientific. There's little harm in taking one of these surveys, other than the time you waste doing so. The results are most often generic and seldom reflect any deep insights into your life or character.

1 Most surveys in your News Feed reflect lifestyle or general interest topics, such as "What color are you?" or "Which celebrity should play you in a movie?" or "What Star Trek character are you?" Click the link to take the survey.

2 The survey itself asks you a series of seemingly unrelated questions, each on its own web page. Make a selection and move to the next page until the survey is completed.

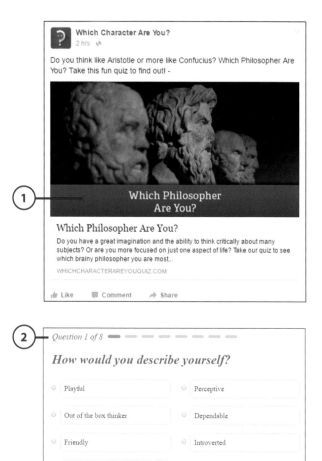

③ At the end of the survey you discover just which superhero you are, or whatever the survey is supposed to determine. You're then prompted to share this earth-shattering information on Facebook. If you click the Facebook button, the survey result is posted to your News Feed for all your friends to see.

Countdown Lists

Another popular type of post is actually common all across the Web, not just on Facebook. This is the quasi-informational post that purports to tell you X number of things about a given topic, in the form of a countdown list. These posts come with sensational headlines designed to grab you and pull you in, such as "18 Reasons We'll Always Be Crazy for Patrick Swayze" or "10 Bad Movie Ideas" or "12 Best Celebrity Beach Bodies."

What these posts do is take you to another website, where each of the X number of things has its own page. You have to click from page to page to view all the items on the countdown list, and each page is chock full of ads. It's all a big scam to get you to click one of the ads (either on purpose or accidentally) so the host site can generate money from that advertising. There's no actual harm done—again, it's just a waste of your time.

Clickbait

Countdown lists and similar posts are often called *clickbait*, because they "bait" you into clicking to learn more. Facebook is trying to crack down on this type of clickbait; if the company is successful, you'll see fewer of these annoying posts in your News Feed.

1 A typical countdown list post starts with an attention-grabbing headline. Click the headline to go to the hosting website, typically in a new browser tab.

2 Each item in the countdown list typically has its own web page, or is part of a long scrolling page. All that space is an opportunity to serve you a plethora of annoying web ads.

BuzzFeed

A surprising number of these countdown clickbait posts link to stories on the BuzzFeed website (www.buzzfeed.com). BuzzFeed is notorious for posting salacious quasi-news stories and multi-page countdown lists—it's a kind of yellow journalism for the Internet age.

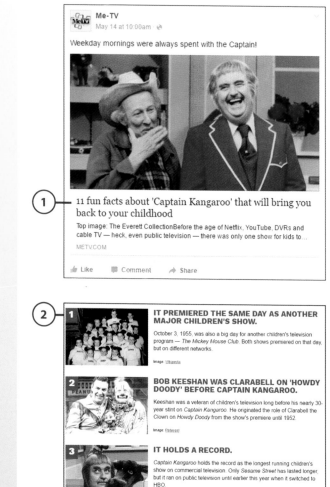

Links to Other Web Pages

Many of your Facebook friends post links to other interesting information on the Web. A post with a web page link is typically accompanied by a thumbnail image from that page, so the post is visual and gets your attention.

1. A post with a link to a web page typically includes an image from that page and the title of that page. Posts can link to traditional web pages or to articles on the Web.

2. Click the image or title of the link and you now see the linked-to web page, typically in a new tab in your web browser. Close that tab to return to Facebook.

Lew Archer
Just now · Lakeville, MN · 🔼

Here's something you'll probably like...

My Windows 10 Computer for Seniors
Book + 2 Hours of Free Video + Content Update Program My Microsoft® Windows® 10 for Seniors is an easy, full-color tutorial on the latest operating system from Microsoft. It includes a DVD with 12 ...

MILLERWRITER.COM

👍 Like   💬 Comment   ➤ Share

It's Not All Good

Think Before You Click

Facebook is like any community—there are always a few charlatans around to trick the naïve or unsuspecting. Beware links that seem too good to be true, such as ads for free iPads, unnecessary PC tune-ups, and the like. Facebook tries to keep these kinds of posts off the site, but isn't always successful. So think twice before you click—and if it smells fishy, don't click at all!

Games

One of the other types of posts you're likely to see a lot comes from the Facebook games that your friends play. These games post your friends' most recent scores and any free items they've won—or even beg you to play the game yourself.

① Posts from Facebook's social games typically include an image from the game and information about your friend's recent play.

② Click the image or button to sign up or play.

Hide Unwanted Posts

If these types of posts annoy you, you can choose to hide them in your News Feed. From the Facebook website, mouse over the post, click the down arrow at the top-right corner, then click Hide All From This Game.

Facebook-Generated Content

In addition to the posts you see from your friends, you'll also find some Facebook-generated content in your News Feed. Facebook likes to remind you of what you've posted and encourages you to share your memories. These posts are most often fun trips down memory lane—based on what you've posted to the Facebook site.

The most common posts you'll see from Facebook are called On This Day. An On This Day post displays a post you've made on this date in a past year, and links to other posts (from other years) you've made on the same date.

Facebook also creates Year in Review posts that you'll see toward the end of any given calendar year. These posts encapsulate your activities over the past year, and are fun to look back on and share with others.

1 Depending on what you've posted and when, you may see an On This Day post in your News Feed. Click or tap See More Memories to view other posts from this date in previous years.

2 Click Share to share an older post with your friends in your current News Feed.

Your Memories on Facebook
Michael, we care about you and the memories you share here. We thought you'd like to look back on this post from 4 years ago.

4 Years Ago

➜ SHARE

SEE MORE MEMORIES — **1**

More Memories

3 Years Ago Today
Sat, May 11, 2013

Michael Miller
May 11, 2013 at 3:56pm ·

Done with jury duty and back to work. An interesting week ensconced in the bowels of the judicial system, now I know why you never see any name actors in the jury on law and order TV shows; we're basically the extras of the production. Still, I enjoyed the many interesting discussions with my fellow jurors, a thoughtful and observant lot. And the bad guy goes to jail – or at least will when the judge sentences him. Justice was served.

➜ Share — **2**

3 To view older posts from this day at any time (on the Facebook website), go to the Apps section of the navigation sidebar and click On This Day.

4 Near the end of each calendar year Facebook generates a Year in Review post for each member. Click any photo to view it as it appeared in its original post.

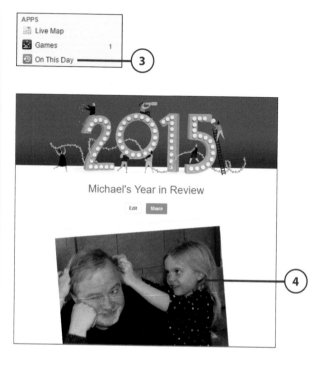

Michael's Year in Review

Suggested Posts

Facebook will, from time to time, post suggested content in your News Feed. These Suggested Posts may be photos, videos, website links, or (more often than not) ads that, based on your previous posts, Facebook thinks you may be interested. Click to read, like, comment on, or share a suggested post. (Or, if it's an ad, just ignore it.)

Trending Topics

As you're discovering, Facebook is a great place to share thoughts and memories with friends and family. It's also a good source of information about what's happening out in the world today.

On the Facebook website, at the top of the right-hand column of the News Feed page, you see a Trending box. This displays topics that are currently being discussed by a lot of Facebook members. Click any topic to view posts about that topic.

In addition, you can search the Facebook site to see what topics are trending, using the Search box in the Facebook website toolbar or at the top of the Facebook mobile app. Again, click or tap any topic to view posts from Facebook members.

1. On the Facebook website, click an icon to view trending topics by category: Top Trends, Politics, Science and Technology, Sports, or Entertainment.

2. Click See More to see more trending topics.

3. Click a topic to view posts about that topic.

4. To search for specific trending topics, click or tap within the Search box and enter your search; matching topics are displayed.

5. If a topic is trending, you'll see the Trending icon. Click or tap this icon to view posts about this topic.

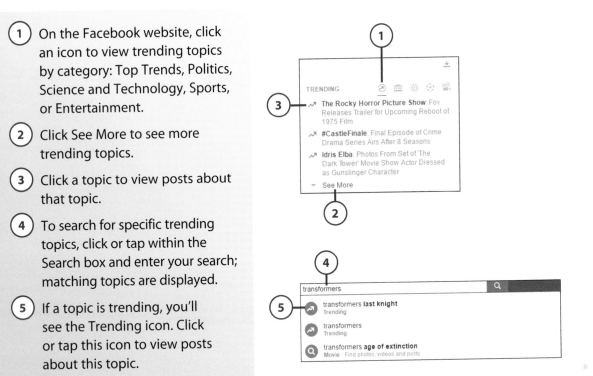

>>>Go Further

THE IMPORTANCE OF SHARING

An increasing number of posts on Facebook are not original posts—they're items that other people have seen on Facebook (and elsewhere) that they've decided to share in their News Feed. This type of sharing is what makes Facebook a social network, and also what can make a given post go viral. When someone shares a post with you and you share it with your friends and they share with their friends—well, you see how quickly something can be spread around.

To share a post you like, click Share beneath the post. You can add your own comments to the post or share it as-is. You can also choose to share the post with your entire friends list (On Your Own Timeline) or with selected friends or groups.

Just try not to share too many of those posts that other people find annoying. The occasional meme or survey is fine and fun in its own way, but if you flood your friends' News Feeds with too many of these frivolous items, you might find that they're not your friends any more.

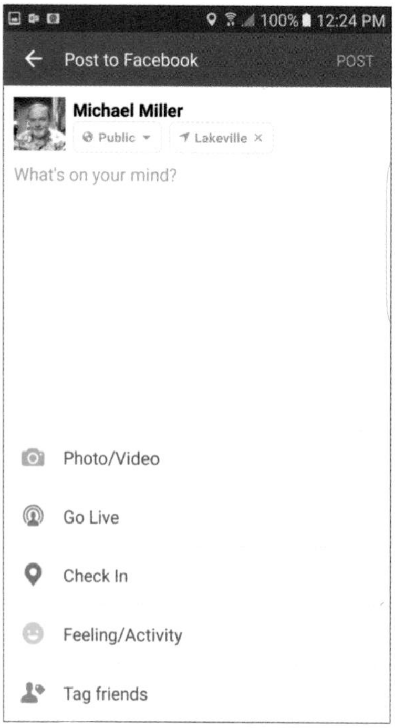
100% 12:24 PM
Post to Facebook
POST
Michael Miller
Public
Lakeville
What's on your mind?
Photo/Video
Go Live
Check In
Feeling/Activity
Tag friends

Photo/Video
Photo Album
What's on your mind?
Public
Post

In this chapter, you learn how to post Facebook status updates for others to read.

→ Updating Your Status
→ Sharing Content from Other Websites

7

Updating Friends and Family on Your Activities

To let your family and friends know what you've been doing and thinking about, you need to post what Facebook calls a *status update*. Every status update you make is broadcast to everyone on your friends list, displayed in the News Feed on their home pages.

Updating Your Status

A status update is, at its most basic, a brief text message. It can be as short as a word or two, or it can be several paragraphs long; that's up to you. (Facebook lets you post updates with more than 60,000 characters, which should be more than long enough for most of us.)

Although a basic status update is all text, you can also attach other items to your status updates, including digital photographs, videos, and links to other web pages. You can also "tag" other Facebook users and groups in your updates, so that their names appear as clickable links (to their Timeline pages).

Tags

A *tag* is a way to mention other Facebook users in your status updates and photos. When a person is tagged in a post, the post appears in that person's Facebook feed, so he knows you're talking about him. In addition, readers can click a tagged name to display that person's Timeline page.

Post a Status Update from the Facebook Mobile App

You can post a status update from the Facebook mobile app or on the Facebook website. It's just as easy either way.

1. Tap the News Feed icon to display the News Feed screen.

2. Tap Status to display the new post screen.

3. Use your device's onscreen keyboard to enter the text of your post in the What's On Your Mind? field.

4. Tap Post when done.

Post a Status Update on the Facebook Website

It's just as easy to post a status update from your notebook or desktop computer, using the Facebook website.

1. Click the Home button on the Facebook toolbar to return to your home page.

2. Click within the Publisher box (labeled What's On Your Mind?) at the top of the page. The Publisher box expands to display a series of option buttons at the bottom.

3. Type your message.

4. Click the Post button when you're done.

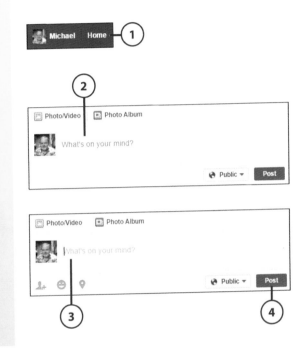

>>>Go Further

HASHTAGS

Facebook offers the option of including *hashtags* in your status updates. A hashtag is like a keyword, a word, or phrase that describes the content of your post—and that readers can click to see similar posts with the same hashtag. A hashtag starts with the hash (#) character, followed by the keyword or phrase (with no spaces between the words). So, for example, a hashtag about this book might look like this: #MyFacebook.

Hashtags were made popular by Twitter, another popular social network. They've never really caught on with Facebook users, however, so you shouldn't bother with including hashtags in your own posts. If you see a hashtag in a friend's status update, you can click it to display a list of other posts that include the same hashtag.

Post a Link to a Web Page

You can include links to other web pages in your status updates. Facebook adds a link to the specified page, and it also lets you include a thumbnail image from that page with the status update.

(1) Start a new post as normal, and enter any accompanying text.

(2) Enter the URL (web address) for the page you want to link to as part of your update.

(3) Facebook should recognize the link and display an image from the website. (If a site has multiple images, you'll see left and right arrows at the top left corner of the image. Click these arrows to select one of multiple images to accompany the link.)

(4) Click the Post button when done.

Delete the URL

If you don't want to display the web page's URL in the body of your status update, you can delete the address after the accompanying image. The link and accompanying image still display under your status update even after you delete the web page URL from your text.

Post a Photograph or Video

Facebook enables you to embed digital photographs and videos in your posts. It's the Facebook equivalent of attaching a file to an email message.

(1) On the Facebook website, go to the Publisher box and click Photo/Video to display the Open dialog box, *or…*

(2) In the Facebook mobile app, tap Photo to display your device's photo gallery.

(3) Navigate to and select the photo or video file(s) you want to upload. You can upload a single video file or multiple photo files. (Tap to select multiple photos on your phone or tablet; to select more than one file on your computer, hold down the Ctrl key while you click each filename.)

(4) Click Open or tap Done.

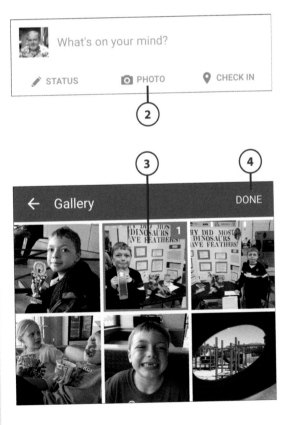

5 You're returned to the Publisher box or screen with your photo(s) added. Click or tap to add your location or another photo, if you want.

6 If you like, enter a short text message describing the photo(s) or video.

7 Click or tap Post.

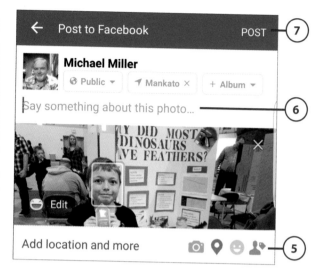

Add Your Location to a Post

Facebook enables you to identify your current location in any post you make. This lets your friends know where you are at any given time.

1 Enter the text of your status update into the Publisher box as normal, or select any photos you want to post.

2 On the Facebook website, click Check In beneath the Publisher box. In the mobile app, tap Add Photos and More, and then tap Check In.

3. If Facebook can tell your location automatically, it displays a list of options. Click or tap to select your current location.

4. If Facebook doesn't display your current location, start entering your location manually; as you type, you see a list of suggested locations.

5. Click or tap the correct location from the resulting list.

6. The location is added to your status update. Click or tap Post.

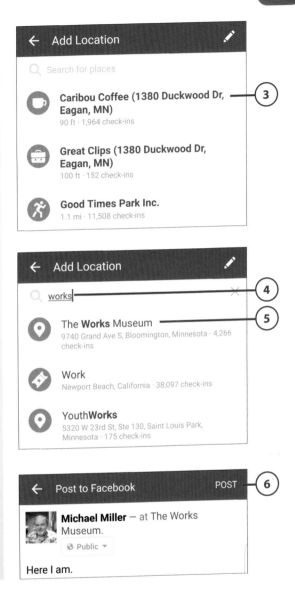

It's Not All Good

Don't Publicize Your Location

You might not want to identify your location on every post you make. If you post while you're away from home, you're letting potential burglars know that your house is empty. You're also telling potential stalkers where they can find you. For these reasons, use caution when posting your location in your status updates.

Tag a Friend in a Post

Sometimes you might want to mention one of your friends in a status update, or include a friend who was with you when the post was made. You can do this by "tagging" friends in your status updates; the resulting post includes a link to the tagged person or persons.

1. Enter the text of your status update into the Publisher box as normal, or any photos you want to post.

2. Click or tap the Tag Friends (Tag People in Your Post) icon beneath the Publisher box.

3. Enter the name of the person you want to tag. As you type, Facebook displays a list with matching names from your Facebook friends list.

4. Select the friend from the list.

5. Click or tap Post.

Tagged Friends

Clicking a tagged person's name in a status update displays the Facebook Timeline page for that person.

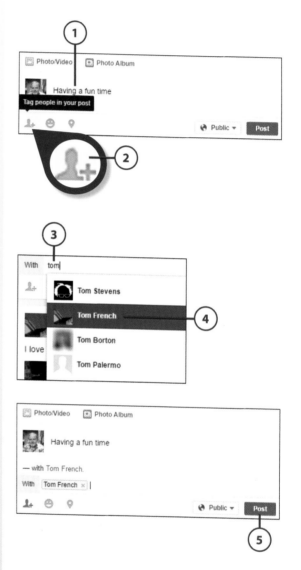

Tell Friends What You're Doing—or How You're Feeling

Given the huge number of posts in which people write about what they're doing at the moment, Facebook has added a What Are You Doing? option to its status updates. This provides a very quick way to tell your friends what you're doing.

1. Enter the text of your status update into the Publisher box as normal. (Or, if you're just posting what you're doing, leave the Publisher box empty.)

2. Click or tap the What Are You Doing? icon beneath the Publisher box.

3. Facebook displays a list of actions. Click or tap the action that best describes what you're doing to display a list of options specific to that action.

4. Select the appropriate option for what you're doing.

5. Your action or feeling is added to your post. Finish the rest of your status update as usual, and then click Post.

Determine Who Can— or Can't—See a Status Update

By default, the items you post to Facebook can be seen by everyone on your friends list. If you'd rather send a given post to a more select group of people, or to everyone on the site, you can change the privacy settings for any individual post. This enables only selected people to see that post; other people on your friends list won't see it at all.

1. Enter the text of your status update, or any photos you want to upload, into the Publisher box as normal.

2. Click or tap the Privacy button or arrow to display a list of privacy options.

3. Click or tap Public to let everyone on Facebook see the post.

4. Click or tap Friends to make a post visible only to people on your friends list.

5. Click or tap Only Me to make the post only visible to yourself—no one else will be able to see it.

6. Click More Options (or tap More on your mobile device) to view more privacy options.

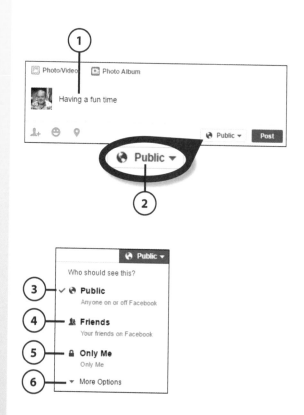

7) In the bottom section of the menu list, click the name of a specific friends list to make a post visible only to the friends on that list.

8) In the mobile app, to select specific individuals who can or can't view this post, tap Friends Except then select specific people or groups.

9) On the Facebook website, to select specific individuals who can or can't view this post, click Custom to display the Custom Privacy panel.

(10) Go to the Don't Share With section and enter names into the These People or Lists box.

(11) Click the Save Changes button. (The privacy options you just set will apply to future posts, as well, until and unless you change them.)

(12) Back in your post, click or tap Post to send this status update to those people you've selected.

Configure Privacy for All Your Posts

Although you can configure the privacy option for each post you make individually, you can also set universal privacy settings that affect all your status updates. Learn more in Chapter 9, "Managing Your Privacy on Facebook."

Custom Privacy ×

+ **Share with**

These people or lists   [Friends ×]

Friends of tagged   ✓

Anyone tagged will be able to see this post.

× **Don't share with**

These people or lists   [   ] ———(10)

Anyone you include here or have on your restricted list won't be able to see this post unless you tag them. We don't let people know when you choose to not share something with them.

Cancel   **Save Changes** ———(11)

🖼 Photo/Video   🖼 Photo Album

Having a fun time

👤 😊 📍   👥 Friends ▾   **Post** ———(12)

>>>Go Further
POSTING ETIQUETTE

Writing a Facebook status update is a bit like sending a text message on your cell phone. As such, status updates do not have to—and often don't—conform to proper grammar, spelling, and sentence structure. It's common to abbreviate longer words, use familiar acronyms, substitute single letters and numbers for whole words, and refrain from all punctuation.

Then there's the issue of how often you should update your Facebook status. Unfortunately, there are no hard and fast rules as to posting frequency. Some people post once a week, others post daily, others post several times a day. In general, you should post when you have something interesting to share—and not because you feel obligated to make a post.

Sharing Content from Other Websites

Facebook is all about sharing things with your friends. Naturally, you can share your thoughts and activities via status updates; you can also upload and share your personal photos and videos.

But Facebook is also connected to many other sites on the Web. This enables you to share content you find elsewhere with your Facebook friends. It's all about posting content from other websites to your Facebook Timeline—and your friends' News Feeds.

Post Content from Another Site

Many websites would like you to share their content with your friends on Facebook. When you're browsing another site and find something interesting to share, look for a Facebook button. This button is sometimes included in a special "sharing" section of the page; it's often labeled Facebook, Facebook Share, Facebook Like, or Facebook Recommend.

News Sharing

Facebook sharing buttons are especially common on news-type sites, which makes it easy to share the articles you find there.

---

(1) Click or tap the Facebook button on the other website. (If you're currently signed into your Facebook account, you probably won't need to log in again. However, if you're prompted to sign into your Facebook account at this point, enter your email address and password, and then click or tap the Log In button.)

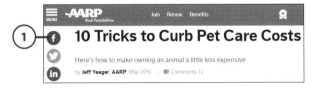

(2)   What you see next depends on the site. In some instances, the link to the page is posted automatically without any comments from you. In other instances, you have the option of including a personal comment with the link; enter your comment, and then click or tap the Share, Share Link, or Post to Facebook button, depending on what you see.

Dinah Lance
Just now

Hayley is coloring Easter eggs!

👍 Like　　💬 Comment　　➤ Share

Dinah Lance
Just now · 🌐

Take a look at our new aquarium. It's a 150 gallon saltwater tank, all ready for a bunch of new fish!

👍 Like　　💬 Comment　　➤ Share

→ What's Good to Post on Facebook
→ What *Not* to Post on Facebook
→ Learning Facebook Etiquette

8

What You Should—and Shouldn't—Share on Facebook

Facebook is not your own private diary or soapbox. It's a public website, where what you post is visible to all your friends and family—and, potentially, millions of other users.

As such, it's important to make your posts interesting to the people who'll be reading them. It's also important not to post certain types of information; with everyone you know—or may know in the future—reading everything you post, it's easy to get yourself in trouble with a few taps of the computer keyboard.

What's Good to Post on Facebook

If you've been on Facebook for any time at all, you've seen your share of boring, self-indulgent, and useless status updates from friends. Not everyone has the knack for posting updates that you really want to read.

It's important to post interesting status updates. But what, exactly, qualifies as something worthwhile to post about?

Post Interesting Information

The best advice I can give for what to post on Facebook is anything that your friends and family are likely to find interesting. Not things you might find interesting, but what others might find interesting about you.

Interesting Topics

To make sure your updates get read, focus on interesting and unique topics. The fact that you went to a concert or read a good book is interesting; that you woke up with a headache or just had a cup of tea is not.

1 Post things you want to share with your Facebook friends. These are moments and events that are not only important to you, but also are things you think your friends might care about, too.

2 Post things that your friends and family want to know about. Friends typically want to know if you've done or seen something interesting, taken a vacation, met a mutual friend, and such. If you think someone's interested in it, post it.

(3) Post about major life events—things in your life that your friends and family *need* to know about. These are important moments and events, such as anniversaries, birthdays, and celebrations.

(4) Post interesting thoughts. Share your wisdom with your friends and family via Facebook status updates—in a noncontroversial, inoffensive way, if you can.

Post Important Information

Many people use Facebook as a kind of bulletin board for their families and friends. One post can inform a large number of people about something important; it's a lot more efficient than sending out dozens of emails or making tons of phone calls. Again—for privacy reasons, be cautious about what you share and with whom.

(1) Post if something has happened to you. If you've been ill or hospitalized, lost your job, moved to a new house, or whatever, use Facebook to let everyone know about it.

(3)
Dinah Lance with Bob Miller.
Just now
Today's our anniversary -- we've been married 10 years now. I've loved every minute of it!

Like   Comment   Share

(4)
Dinah Lance
Just now
It seems to me that the best way to solve this thing is to work together instead of arguing over the small points.

Like   Comment   Share

Write a comment...

(1)
Dinah Lance
Just now
Okay, it's happening. I'm leaving the Friendship Matters organization next week for an exciting new position at the First Light company. It's hard to leave, but I'm really looking forward to all the opportunities at First Light. Wish me luck!

Like   Comment   Share

(2) Post if something has happened to your spouse or partner. Many of your friends are likely mutual friends, so if anything major has happened, include that information in your status update—especially if your spouse or partner can't post, for whatever reason.

(3) Post if something has happened to another family member. You might know something about a cousin or nephew that others in your family might not know about. Share your information with other family members via a Facebook post.

(4) Post if something has happened to a mutual friend. It's tough to keep track of all your old friends. Start the chain going by posting what you know, and let your other friends pass it on to their friends, too.

> **Dinah Lance**
> Just now
>
> For all of Bob's friends out there, he hasn't posted for a few days because he's been in the hospital. Nothing major, he took a fall off a ladder while cleaning the gutters and broke his leg. He's home now and will be up and hobbling around in no time. Just wanted to let everybody know what was happening.
>
> 👍 Like   💬 Comment   ➡ Share   (2)

> **Dinah Lance**
> Just now
>
> Ran into my cousin Elbert last night at the mall. Haven't seen him in awhile, wanted to let everybody know that he's doing fine, still working at the tire store. He and Marlene are planning on getting married next spring, no date set yet. He's looking good, and it was good to catch up with him.
>
> 👍 Like   💬 Comment   ➡ Share   (3)

> **Dinah Lance**
> Just now
>
> Some of you might remember Ginger who used to work in the office about five or six years ago. I heard that she and Jim broke up and she's moving back into the area. I'll let you know more when I hear from her.
>
> 👍 Like   💬 Comment   ➡ Share   (4)

What *Not* to Post on Facebook

There are some things you probably shouldn't post on Facebook. Many of the posts you see from friends are mundane and uninteresting; some are inflammatory and offensive. And then there are those posts that just contain too much information about personal matters you'd rather not know.

It's important, then, to think before you post. Remember that Facebook is not a private diary; it's a public website with more than 1 billion users. Some things simply shouldn't be shared with all those people.

Avoid Uninteresting or Unwise Posts

By default, all your Facebook friends will see everything you post. Post only that information that you'd want your friends (or spouse or grandkids) to read.

- Don't complain. The last thing your Facebook friends want to find in their News Feeds is your private griping. It's okay to grouse and be grumpy from time to time (you're entitled), but don't use Facebook as your personal forum for petty grievances. If you have a personal problem, deal with it; whining gets old really fast. (We especially don't want to hear if you're having a fight with your partner or problems with your kids. This sort of thing is best kept private.)

- Keep your opinions to yourself. In particular, avoid getting overly political or controversial in your posts. It's true that some people like to use Facebook as a platform for their opinions, but that's a sure fire way to get "unfriended" by people who disagree with you. Although it might be okay to share your opinions with close real-world friends, spouting off in a public forum is not only bad form; it's a way to incite a flame war—an unnecessary online war of words.

- Don't post confessions. Facebook is not the place to come clean about past indiscretions; it's a public forum, not a private confessional. If you need to confess something to someone, do it in a more private way.

- Don't get too personal. Facebook is definitely not the best place to share intimate details about your life. Most people feel a little awkward when someone discloses just a little too much about his or her personal life. A good rule of thumb is that if you don't want your kids or grandkids to know about it, don't share it on Facebook.

- Don't post anything that anyone—including lawyers, employers, or the police—could use against you. When you post a status update, it's there for everyone to see, friend or foe. It gets back to that confessional thing; if you think something could come back to bite you, don't post it.

- Don't post embarrassing photos of yourself or others, and don't tag anyone else who might be in those photos—especially your children or grandchildren. You don't want to humiliate yourself or your family online.

- Don't post just to get attention. Here's something new to Facebook: *vague-booking*. This is the practice of posting a message that's intentionally vague but hints at some personal problem or crisis (such as "Life is so unfair. You know who I'm talking about."). People vaguebook to get their friends to respond with worried inquiries about what's wrong; it's highly manipulative and sure to create enmity over time. If you really have some sort of problem, it's better to call a friend instead of posting about it publicly to everyone on Facebook.

- Don't post if you don't have anything interesting to say. Posting too many meaningless updates will cause friends to start ignoring everything you post.

Avoid Posting Personal Information

There's a whole other class of information you shouldn't post on Facebook—personal information that could be used by identity thieves to hijack your bank accounts or site memberships online. If you don't want to become a victim of identity theft, avoid posting too many personal details to your Facebook account.

- *Don't* post your personal contact information—phone number, street address, email address, and so forth. (And edit your profile so that this contact info is private, not public.) You don't want complete strangers to contact or harass you.

- *Don't* post location information when you're away from home. This can tip off burglars that your house is empty, or notify stalkers where you can be found. Wait until after you get home to share where you had dinner or vacationed.

- *Don't* post the layout of your house. You don't want to give potential burglars a roadmap to all your goodies.

- *Don't* post your Social Security number (SSN). Ever. If your SSN gets in the wrong hands, identity theft will result.

- *Don't* post other pieces of information that could be used to gain access to your online accounts—your birthdate, birthplace, mother's maiden name, and so forth. This information is typically used for "challenge questions" if you forget your password on a website; if you post this information where potential thieves can see it, they might be able to reset your password and gain access to your online accounts.

Learning Facebook Etiquette

Your status updates on Facebook should be not only interesting but also easy to read. Not that each post has to be letter perfect, but there are some guidelines you should follow.

Carefully Compose Your Status Updates

Facebook status updates are not long, thought-out missives. A status update is more immediate than an email, and less well-constructed than a handwritten letter.

That said, more people will read your posts if you follow some simple guidelines. Your status updates don't have to be perfect, but they do need to be in the ballpark.

- Be personal and personable. Your writing on Facebook should be light and informal, not stiff and professional. Write as you'd talk, in your own personal voice. Make it sound like you—and be as friendly as you know how to be.

- Keep your posts short. Facebook users, even your dear old friends, don't have the attention span, the patience, or the inclination to read long tomes. They want quick bits of information, something they can scan without necessarily reading. Keep each status update to a paragraph, no more than a few sentences—and the shorter the better.

- Include links and photos in your posts. A Facebook status update doesn't have to be just text. You can—and should—include photos and links to other websites in your posts. In fact, most posts today have some sort of visual element. Nothing wrong with text-only posts; it's just that users are drawn to—and tend to expect—more visually interesting posts. This means that people are more likely to ignore text-only posts in favor of posts with some sort of image. If you can illustrate your point with a photo, or a link to a picture on another web page, then do so.

Know the Shorthand

As anyone of a younger generation will no doubt attest, writing a Facebook status update is a bit like sending a text message on your cell phone. You do it quickly, without a lot of preparation or editing. It's an in-the-moment communication, and as such you can't be expected to take the time to create a grammatically perfect message.

For this reason, Facebook status updates do not have to—and seldom do—conform to proper grammar, spelling, and sentence structure. It's common to abbreviate longer words, use familiar acronyms, substitute single letters and numbers for whole words, and refrain from all punctuation.

For example, instead of spelling out the word "Friday," you can just write "Fri." Instead of saying "See you later," just say "later." Instead of spelling out "New York City," use the abbreviation "NYC."

Misspellings

It's also acceptable, at least to some users, to have the occasional misspelling. It's not something I personally like to do or see, but I'm a professional writer and pickier about these things than many people; most people will let it slide if you get the spelling or grammar wrong once in a while.

Younger users, especially, like to use a sort of online shorthand (or "Facebook grammar") to pack as much as possible into a short status update. These are the same acronyms and abbreviations that have been used for decades in text messaging, instant messaging, and Internet chat rooms. You might not be familiar with this shorthand, much of which is detailed in Table 8.1. It may be a tad unseemly for older folks to use this hip lingo, but it certainly helps to know what everything means when you're reading posts from your kids or grandkids.

Table 8.1   Common Facebook Acronyms

Acronym	Description
AFAIK	As far as I know
ASAP	As soon as possible
ASL	Age/sex/location
B/W	Between
B4	Before
BC	Because
BFN	Bye for now
BR	Best regards
BRB	Be right back
BTW	By the way
CU	See you
Cuz	Because
FB	Facebook
FTF	Face to face
FWIW	For what it's worth
FYI	For your information
GM	Good morning
GN	Good night
HTH	Hope that helps
IDK	I don't know
IM	Instant message
IMHO	In my humble opinion
IRL	In real life
JK	Just kidding
K	Okay
L8	Late
L8r	Later
LMAO	Laughing my ass off

Acronym	Description
LMK	Let me know
LOL	Laughing out loud
NSFW	Not safe for work
OH	Overheard
OMG	Oh my God
Pls *or* Plz	Please
Ppl *or* peeps	People
R	Are
Rly	Really
ROFL	Rolling on the floor laughing
SD	Sweet dreams
Tht	That
Thx *or* Tnx	Thanks
TY	Thank you
TTYL	Talk to you later
U	You
Ur	Your
WTF	What the f**k
WTH	What the hell
YMMV	Your mileage may vary
YW	You're welcome
Zzz	Sleeping

>>>*Go Further*

HOW OFTEN SHOULD YOU POST?

How often should you update your Facebook status? That's an interesting question, without a defined answer.

Some of my Facebook friends post frequently—several times a day. Some only post occasionally, once a month or so. Most, however, post once a day or once every few days. So if there's an average, that's it.

Some of the more frequent posters are justified, in that they post a lot of interesting information. Other frequent posters I find more annoying, in that their posts are more personal and less practical; every little tic and burp is immortalized in its own update. That's probably posting too much.

On the other hand, my friends who only post once a month or so probably aren't trying hard enough. I'd like to hear from them more often; certainly they're doing something interesting that's worth posting about. After a while, I tend to forget that they're still around.

So you need to post often enough that your friends don't forget about you, but not so often that they wish you'd just shut up. I suppose your update frequency has something to do with what it is you're doing, and how interesting that is. But it's okay to post just to let people know you're still there—as long as you don't do so hourly.

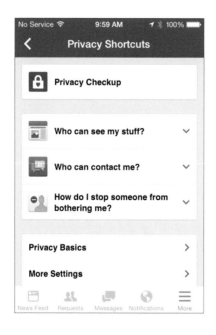

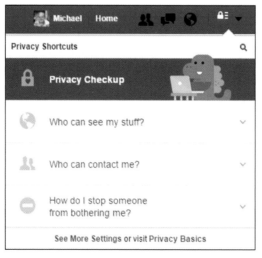

→ Determining Who Sees What You Post
→ Limiting Contact from Other Members
→ Controlling Tagging
→ Controlling Who Sees What on Your Timeline

Managing Your Privacy on Facebook

Facebook is a social network, and being social means sharing one's personal information with others. In Facebook's case, it's likely that you're sharing a lot of your private information not just with your friends but also with Facebook and its partners and advertisers.

Unfortunately, all this sharing poses a problem if you'd rather keep some things private. If you share everything with everyone, all sorts of information can get out—and be seen by people you don't want to see it. Keeping personal information personal on Facebook is possible, but it requires some work on your part.

Determining Who Sees What You Post

Many people worry about their privacy online, and for good reason. Not only are there a lot of companies that would like to get hold of your private information to contact you for advertising and promotional reasons, but the Internet is also rife with identify thieves eager to steal your private information for their own nefarious means.

This is why some people are cautious about getting on Facebook; they're afraid that the information they post will be needlessly shared with the wrong people. There's a basis to these fears, as Facebook likes to share all your information with just about everybody on its social network—not just your friends or their friends, but also advertisers and third-party websites.

Fortunately, you can configure Facebook to be much less public than it could be—and thus keep your private information private. You just have to know which settings to tweak.

Configure Facebook's Default Privacy Settings

The first step to ensuring your Facebook privacy is to determine who, by default, can see all the posts you make. You can do this in a positive fashion, by telling Facebook precisely who can view your new posts. You can also take a more defensive approach, by telling Facebook who *can't* see your status updates.

Default Sharing

Facebook's default sharing settings used to be Public, meaning that all your information and status updates were shared with everyone. Fortunately, that's not the case anymore. Today, Facebook sets the default sharing setting for all new users as Friends, meaning your posts and profile information are visible only to those users on your friends list. (If you signed up for Facebook prior to May 2014, your default privacy setting might still be set as Public.)

1. In the Facebook mobile app, tap the More (three line) icon, then scroll down and tap Privacy Shortcuts. *Or…*

2. On the Facebook website, click the Privacy Shortcuts button on the Facebook toolbar to display the pull-down menu.

3. Click or tap the down arrow next to Who Can See My Stuff? to expand the menu.

4. Go to the Who Can See My Future Posts? section, click or tap the down or right arrow, and select one of the resulting options.

5. Click or tap Public to let anyone on Facebook see your posts.

6. Click or tap Friends to restrict viewing to only people on your Facebook friends list.

7. Click or tap Only Me to keep your posts totally private—that is, to keep anyone from seeing them.

8. If you're configuring privacy on the Facebook website, you have more options available, so click More Options to further expand the menu.

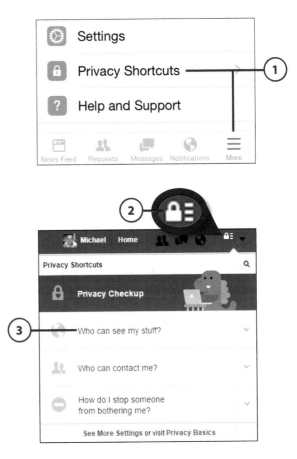

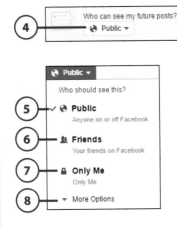

9 Click Custom to create a custom list of people who can or can't see your posts. The Custom Privacy panel displays.

10 In the Share With box, enter the names of friends or groups of friends you want to share with.

11 To share with friends of people you tag in your posts or photos, check the Friends of Tagged option.

12 To *not* share your posts with a given friend or group of friends, enter that name into the Don't Share With box.

13 Click the Save Changes button.

> 👤 Friends except Acquaintances
> ✳ Custom ——— **9**

Custom Privacy ✕

➕ **Share with** ——— **10**

These people or lists   Friends ✕

Friends of tagged   ✓ ——— **11**
Anyone tagged will be able to see this post

✕ **Don't share with**

These people or lists ——— **12**

Anyone you include here or have on your restricted list won't be able to see this post unless you tag them. We don't let people know when you choose to not share something with them.

Cancel **Save Changes** ——— **13**

Select Who Can See (or Not See) Individual Posts

Even after you set these global posting privacy settings, you can change the privacy setting for any individual post you make. That is, any given post can be sent to a specific list of people that overrides the global settings you made previously.

For example, you might have set your global privacy settings so that your friends can see your posts. But if you have a new post that you only want your immediate family to see, you can configure that single post to go only to your family members, not to everyone else on your friends list.

Note, however, that when you reset privacy settings for a given post, those new settings remain in effect for all future posts—until you change them again.

1 Go to your Facebook Home page and start a new status update as normal. Click or tap the Post Privacy Setting button to display the menu of options.

2 Click or tap Public to make this post visible to any Facebook user.

3 Click or tap Friends to make this post visible to everyone on your friends list.

4 Click or tap Only Me to keep your posts totally private—that is, to keep anyone from seeing them.

5 On the Facebook website, click More Options to further expand the menu.

6 Click Custom to display the Custom Privacy panel.

7 Select the necessary options to make this post visible to or hide it from specific people or groups of friends.

8 Click the Save Changes button. This new setting applies for all future posts—until you change it again.

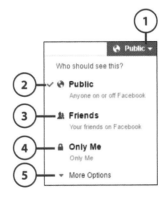

1

Public ▾

Who should see this?

2 ✓ **Public**
Anyone on or off Facebook

3 **Friends**
Your friends on Facebook

4 **Only Me**
Only Me

5 More Options

6 Friends except Acquaintances

Custom

Custom Privacy ✕

7

+ **Share with**

These people or lists [Friends ✕]

Friends of tagged ✓

Anyone tagged will be able to see this post

✕ **Don't share with**

These people or lists

Anyone you include here or have on your restricted list won't be able to see this post unless you tag them. We don't let people know when you choose to not share something with them.

Cancel **Save Changes**

8

Limiting Contact from Other Members

Are you getting private messages or friend requests from people you don't know? It's time to reconfigure your privacy settings to limit contact from complete strangers.

Control Who Can Send You Friend Requests

You can limit who on Facebook can request to be your friend. By default, anyone on Facebook can friend you; you might not want to see friend requests from people you don't know, however.

(1) In the Facebook mobile app, tap the More (three line) icon, and then scroll down and tap Privacy Shortcuts. Or...

(2) On the Facebook website, click the Privacy Shortcuts button to display the drop-down menu.

(3) Click or tap the down arrow next to Who Can Contact Me? to expand this section.

(4) Click Who Can Send Me Friend Requests and make a selection—Everyone (the default) or Friends of Friends.

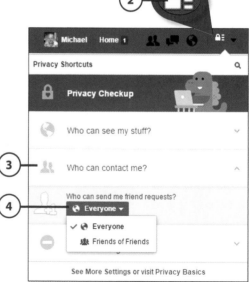

Controlling Tagging

Facebook likes to connect people with each other. This is often done via "tagging," where one user can tag ("who are you with?") another user in a status update or photo without asking the other person. When you're tagged, you're connected to that post or photo, whether you want to be or not—which can be an invasion of your privacy.

Restrict Who Sees Tag Suggestions in Photos That Look Like You

One of the ways that Facebook encourages tagging is by suggesting people to tag when someone posts a photo. Facebook does this via facial recognition technology; it compares a given photo with the millions of other photos uploaded to its site and tries to match a new face with one it already knows.

So if someone uploads a picture of someone who looks like you, Facebook suggests that you be tagged in that photo. That's fine, unless that's not really you—or if the photo is one you'd rather not be associated with. Fortunately, you can turn off these photo tag suggestions.

It's Not All Good

You Can Still Be Tagged

Just because you turn off Facebook's ability to suggest your name when someone uploads a photo, that doesn't mean you can't be tagged in that photo. The person who uploaded the photo can still manually tag you, even if your name isn't automatically suggested.

① In the Facebook mobile app, tap the More icon then scroll down and tap Account Settings (Android) or Settings, Account Settings (iOS) to open the Settings screen. *Or...*

⚙ Settings ——————————————① ①

🔒 Privacy Shortcuts ›

❓ Help and Support

News Feed   Requests   Messages   Notifications   More

(2) On the Facebook website, click the down arrow button at the far right of the Facebook toolbar to display the menu of options, and then click Settings to display the Account Settings page.

(3) Click or tap Timeline and Tagging.

(4) Go to the How Can I Manage Tags People Add and Tagging Suggestions? section.

(5) Go to the Who Sees Tag Suggestions When Photos That Look Like You Are Uploaded? option and tap the right arrow or click Edit.

(6) By default, Friends is selected, which means that all of your friends will see your name in their tag suggestions. Click or tap No One to keep your name from appearing as a tag suggestion for anyone, including your friends. (And if you're doing this on the Facebook website, you need to click Close after making your selection.)

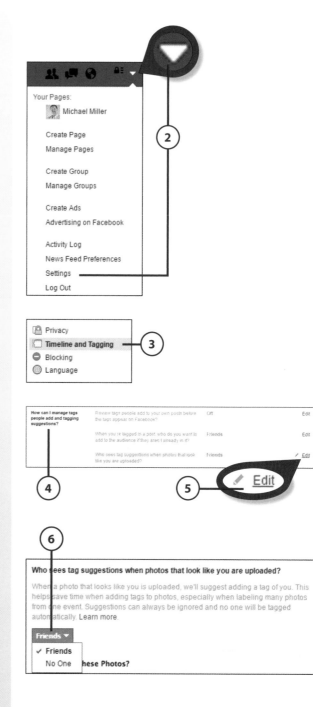

Limit Who Can See Posts You're Tagged In

As noted, there's nothing to stop friends from manually tagging you in the posts they make and the photos they upload. What you can do, however, is keep anyone else from seeing those tags—in effect, hiding your name when tagged.

1. From the Timeline and Tagging (Settings) page, go to the Who Can See Things on My Timeline? section.

2. Go to the Who Can See Posts You've Been Tagged In On Your Timeline? option and tap the right arrow or click Edit.

3. Click or tap the privacy button and select Friends of Friends to limit your exposure to people on your friends list and their Facebook friends.

4. Click or tap Friends to limit your exposure to only people on your friends list.

5. Click Only Me to hide your name from everyone on Facebook. (And if you're doing this on the Facebook website, you need to click Close after making your selection.)

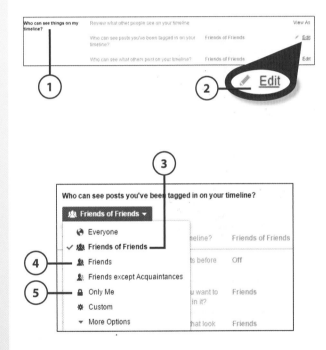

Approve Tags People Add to Your Posts

Here's a real invasion of your privacy. You post a picture to Facebook, and someone tags himself in your photo—even if it's not really a picture of him! Fortunately, Facebook gives you the option of reviewing all tags that people add to the posts you make and the photos you upload—so you can restrict who "associates" with you online.

1. From the Timeline and Tagging (Settings) page, go to the How Can I Manage Tags People Add and Tagging Suggestions? section.

2. Go to the Review Tags People Add to Your Own Posts Before the Tags Appear on Facebook? option and tap the right arrow or click Edit.

3. On the Facebook website, click the Disabled button, select Enabled, and then click Close. You are now notified whenever someone tries to add his or her tag to one of your posts or photos, and you have the option of approving or rejecting that tag. *Or…*

4. In the mobile app, tap the Enabled (Android) or Tag Review (iOS) switch to move it to On.

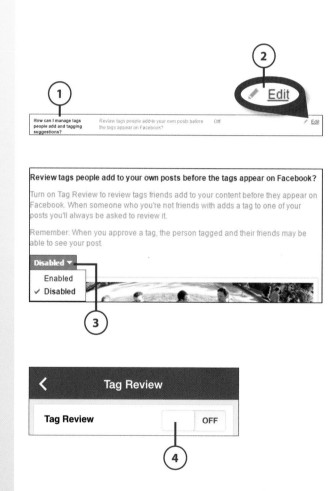

Controlling Who Sees What on Your Timeline

Another place that Facebook displays personal information is on your Timeline. Fortunately, you can limit who can see specific information there. This is best accomplished from the Facebook website.

Control Who Sees Specific Information

Any given section in your Timeline has its own privacy settings. That is, you can configure different parts of your Timeline to be visible to different groups of people. For example, you can configure your Timeline so that everyone on Facebook can see your About section, but limit viewing of your Photos section to only people on your friends list.

1. From your Timeline page, click the Update Info button.

2. In the left column, select the type of information you want to configure.

3. Mouse over the individual item you want to change, and then click that item's Privacy button.

4. Select who can see this information: Public (everyone on Facebook), Friends (people on your friends list), Only Me (no one can see it), Custom, or one of your customized friends lists.

5. Click Save Changes.

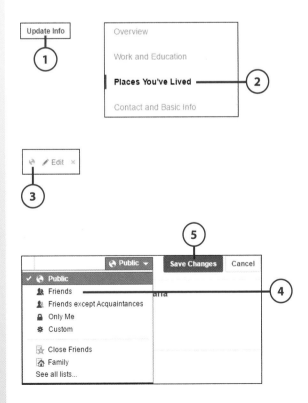

Q Search

Sherry 'French Elliott' Miller added 5
new photos to the album: **Summer 2016**
— with **Kristi 'Elliott' Lee** and **Amy
Elliott**.
May 29 at 8:08pm · 🌐

👍❤😮 Roger Lee and 41 others · 1 Comment

👍 Like · 💬 Comment · ➤ Share

Michael Miller in 📍Burnsville, Minnesota
May 24 at 5:32pm · 🌐

Last week Kristi 'Elliott' Lee and her kids moved out of our basement to their
own apartment. That's a great step forward for them, even if that means we
see them less and our house is a lot quieter. On the plus side, after too
many years to count, I finally have my drum room back!

👍 Like · 💬 Comment · ➤ Share

In this chapter, you find out how to view photos and videos that your friends have shared on Facebook, as well as how to upload your own photos and videos for your friends to see.

→ Viewing Friends' Photos and Videos
→ Sharing Your Photos and Videos with Friends

Viewing and Sharing Photos and Videos

Sharing pictures and home movies is a great way to show your friends and family what you've been up to. Everybody loves looking at pictures, still or moving—whether they're vacation photos or home movies of your cute kids or grandkids.

It should come as no surprise that Facebook is the largest photo-sharing site on the Internet. (It's pretty big for sharing videos, too.) It's easy to upload photos or videos to a Facebook photo album and then share them with all your Facebook friends. It's equally easy to view your friends' photos and videos on Facebook—and download and print those photos you'd like to keep for posterity.

Viewing Friends' Photos and Videos

Some people on Facebook post photos and videos as part of their regular status updates. These items appear in your News Feed, as part of the stream of your friends' status updates.

Other Facebook users upload their photos to special photo albums they've created in their Facebook accounts. This is a more serious and organized way to share a large number of photos online. You can view these photo albums from the user's Timeline page.

View Photos in Your News Feed

When a friend posts a photo as part of a status update, that photo appears in your News Feed. You can view photos at that small size within the News Feed, or enlarge them to view them full screen.

1. Within your News Feed, all photos appear within the bodies of the accompanying status updates. To view a larger version of any picture, click or tap the photo in the post.

2. If you're using the Facebook website, this displays the photo within its own *lightbox*—a special window superimposed over the News Feed. To view the photo even larger, click the Enter Fullscreen icon at the top-right corner of the photo. (To exit fullscreen mode, press Esc on your computer keyboard or the X at the top-right corner of the screen.)

(3) If you're using the Facebook mobile app, you see the photo on its own photo page. Swipe up from the bottom of the screen to return to the News Feed. (Or, in the iOS app, tap the X in the upper-left corner.)

View a Video in Your News Feed

Any videos that your friends upload to Facebook also show up in your News Feed. You'll see a video as a thumbnail image with a playback arrow on top; playing the video is as easy as clicking that image.

YouTube Videos

Users can also share videos they find on YouTube, Vimeo, and other video sharing sites. These videos also appear in your friends' News Feeds. To view the video on the YouTube or Vimeo site, click or tap the video's title to open that site in a new tab in your web browser, or in the appropriate app on your mobile device. (Click or tap the video itself and it plays in the News Feed.)

(1) Navigate to the status update that contains the video, and click or tap the video thumbnail to play the video. In some cases, video playback begins in the News Feed itself. In other cases, playback begins in a separate video player similar to Facebook's photo lightbox. (The video may play automatically when you scroll to the post, but without sound—kind of like a muted preview. If this is the case, you need to click or tap the video to play it back with sound.)

Auto Playback

To turn auto playback on or off on the Facebook website, go to the Settings page, select the Videos tab on the left, then click the button next to the Auto-Play Videos option. Select On to always play videos or Off to never engage Auto-Play.

(2) To view the video at a larger size on the Facebook website, mouse over the video to display the playback controls at the bottom and click the Full Screen icon. Press Esc on your computer keyboard to return to normal playback mode.

3 To pause the playback on the Facebook website, mouse over the video to display the playback controls, and then click the Pause button—which now changes to a Play button. To pause the playback in the Android mobile app, just tap the screen. (In the iOS app, you have to tap the Pause button.) Click or tap the Play button or tap the screen again to resume playback.

4 Click and drag the volume control to raise or lower the playback volume on the Facebook website. (If you're using the mobile app, use your phone's up and down volume buttons to raise or lower the playback volume.)

5 Click and drag (or tap and drag) the time slider to move to another point in the video.

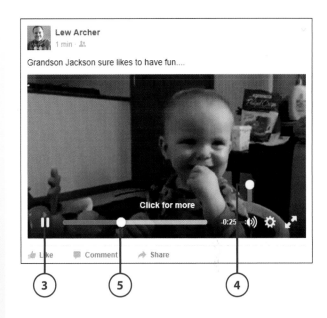

Lew Archer
1 min

Grandson Jackson sure likes to have fun....

Click for more

-0:25

Like   Comment   Share

3   **5**   **4**

View a Friend's Photo Albums

More serious photographers—and people with a lot of photos to share—organize their Facebook photos into individual photo albums. These are virtual versions of those traditional photo albums you've kept in the past. You can then navigate through a friend's photo albums to find and view the photos you like.

1. Click or tap your friend's name or profile picture anywhere on Facebook to open his Timeline page.

2. Click or tap Photos to display your friend's Photos page.

3. Click or tap Photos of *Friend* to view all photos of your friend.

4. Click *Friend's* Photos (or tap Uploads) to view all photos posted by your friend.

5. Click or tap Albums to view photos as posted in their photo albums.

6. Click or tap to open the selected album, then click or tap any photo to view it in the photo viewer.

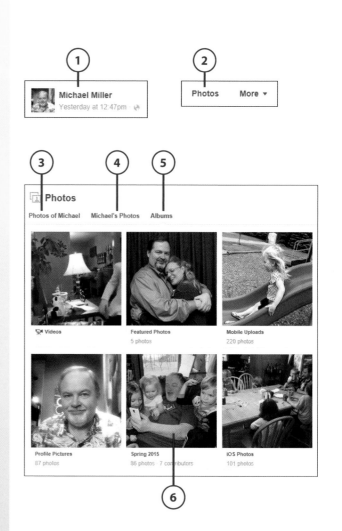

View All of a Friend's Videos

All the videos a friend has uploaded are displayed in a Videos album on the Albums tab of the friend's Photos page. You can play back any video from here.

1 Go to your friend's Photos page and click or tap Albums to display your friend's photo albums.

2 Click or tap the Videos album to display all this person's videos.

Upload Order
The videos in the Videos album are organized by date uploaded. Newest uploads are displayed first.

---

3 Click or tap a video thumbnail to play that video.

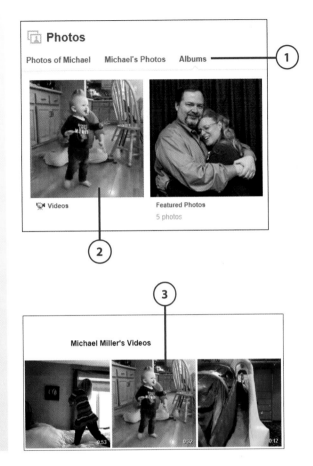

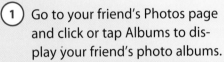

>>>Go Further

LIKING, COMMENTING ON, AND SHARING PHOTOS AND VIDEOS

You can like, comment on, and even share your friends' photos and videos. There are a number of ways to do these things.

If the photo or video appears in your News Feed, you can comment, like, or share it just as you would a normal status update. Just click or tap the appropriate link and proceed as normal.

You can also perform any of these actions from the photo or video viewer page. Again, click or tap Like, Comment, or Share to do what you want to do.

Tag Yourself in a Friend's Photo

If you find yourself in a photo that a friend has taken and uploaded to Facebook, you can "tag" yourself in that photo. When you're tagged in a photo, that photo appears in your Facebook timeline, in your friends' News Feeds, and on your Facebook photo albums page, on the Photos of You tab. This is easiest to do on the Facebook website, using your web browser.

(1) Display the photo in the photo viewer, mouse over the photo to display the menu at the bottom of the photo, and then click Tag Photo.

(2) Mouse over your face in the photo. A box appears around your face, with a text box underneath.

(3) Click within the text box to display a list of suggested names. Click your name in the list (it's probably the first one listed), or enter your name into the text box.

(4) Your name is now tagged to your face in this photo. Click Done Tagging to finish.

It's Not All Good

Removing Your Name from a Photo—Or Removing a Photo

You might not want to be tagged in a given picture. Perhaps the photo shows you doing something you shouldn't be doing. Maybe the photo is just a bad picture you don't particularly like. Or maybe you just don't like your name or face being out there on the Internet without your permission. In any instance, Facebook enables you to remove your name from any photo tagged by a friend; you can even request that a given photo be completely removed from the Facebook site.

To do this, display the photo and mouse over the photo to display the menu at the bottom of the photo. Click Options and then click Remove Tag; this displays the Remove Tag panel.

To remove your tag from the photo, click Okay.

Download a Photo

If you find a friend's photo that you really like, you can download it to your own computer, for your own personal use.

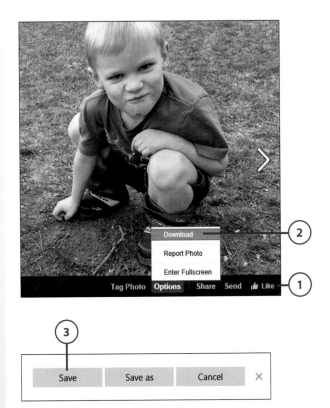

1. Display the photo in the photo viewer and mouse over the photo to display the menu at the bottom of the photo.

2. Click Options, and then click Download.

3. Click Save if you're prompted to open or save the file. (If you don't see this prompt, the photo is automatically saved to the Downloads folder on your computer.)

4 If you see the Save As dialog box, select where you want to save the file, and then click the Save button.

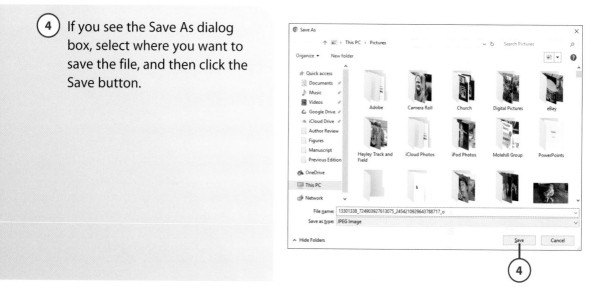

Sharing Your Photos and Videos with Friends

Whether you take pictures and videos with your smartphone, tablet, or digital camera, you can share them all on Facebook with your friends and family. You can share directly from your mobile device or from your computer—after you've transferred your photos to your PC, of course.

Share a Photo or Video in a Status Update on the Facebook Website

Facebook lets you share any photo or video as a status update, which means all your friends should see them in their News Feeds. Your uploaded photos and videos also end up on your Photos page, accessible from your Timeline for all your friends to view.

We'll look first at how to upload photos and videos from your computer, using the Facebook website.

(1) From the News Feed page, go to the Publisher box and click Photo/Video to display the Open dialog box.

(2) Navigate to and select the photo or video file(s) you want to upload. You can upload a single video file or multiple photo files. (Tap to select multiple photos on your phone or tablet; to select more than one file on your computer, hold down the Ctrl key while you click each filename.)

(3) Click Open or tap Done.

(4) You're returned to the Publisher box or screen with your photo(s) added. Click to add another picture, if you want.

(5) If you like, enter a short text message describing the photo(s) or video.

(6) Click Post.

Processing Videos

When you upload a video, Facebook must process it into the proper format to distribute on its site. This might take several minutes. You should be informed when the processing is complete; you can then edit the video description if you like, or select a thumbnail image for longer videos.

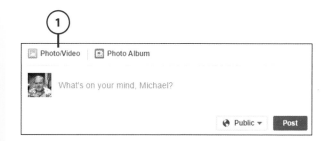

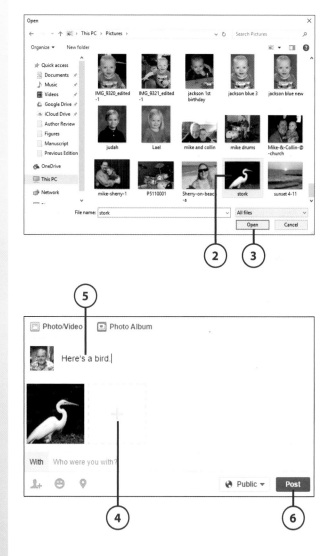

Share a Photo or Video from Your Mobile Phone

If you use your mobile phone to take photos, it's even easier to post those photos to Facebook. You don't have to transfer your phone photos to your computer first (although you can); Facebook lets you upload photos directly from your phone, using Facebook's mobile app. (This example uses Facebook's Android app; the iOS app works similarly.)

1. Use your phone's camera to take a picture and then tap to open that picture in your phone's photo or gallery app.

2. Tap Share.

3. Tap Facebook.

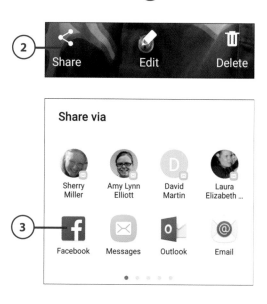

4 Say something about this photo, if you want.

5 Tap Post to post the photo as a status update.

Uploading from the Gallery

You can also upload photos you've taken previously, from your phone's picture gallery. Just navigate to and open the photo you want to post, then tap Share and proceed from there.

Upload Photos to a New Photo Album

If you have a lot of photos to share on Facebook, the best approach is to create a series of virtual photo albums. This enables you to organize your photos by topic or date. For example, you might create an album for Summer Vacation, Thanksgiving 2016, Grandkids, or Retirement Party. Organizing your photos into albums also makes it easier for your friends to find specific photos.

This task is most easily done on the Facebook website, from your computer.

1 From your Timeline page, click Photos to display your Photos page.

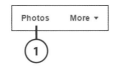

(2) Click the Create Album button to display the Open dialog box.

(3) Select the photo(s) you want to upload.

(4) Click the Open button to see the Untitled Album page.

Selecting Multiple Photos

It's easy to upload more than one photo at a time. Just hold down the Ctrl key while clicking files to select multiple files.

(5) Click Untitled Album and enter the desired album title. (Note that this page looks slightly different in different browsers; I'm showing it in Google Chrome.)

(6) Click Say Something About This Album and enter an album description.

Optional Information

All the information you can add to a photo album is entirely optional; you can add as much or as little as you like. You don't even have to add a title—if you don't, Facebook uses the title Untitled Album.

7 Enter a location in the Where Were These Taken? box to enter a geographic location for all the photos in this album. (You can later change the location for any specific photo, as noted in Step 12.)

8 Check the High Quality option to upload these photos at a quality suitable for printing. Leave this box unchecked if the photos will only be viewed onscreen.

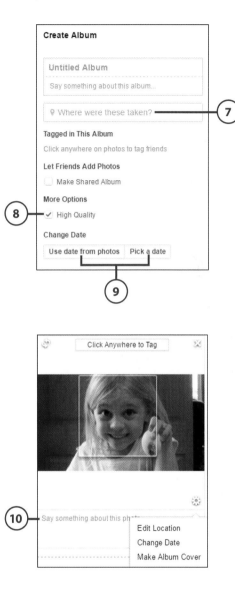

High-Quality Photos

For best possible picture quality for anyone downloading or printing your photos, check the High Quality option to upload and store your photos at their original resolution. Note, however, that it takes longer to upload high-quality photos than those in standard quality.

9 In the Change Date section, opt to either Use Date from Photos (each photo retains its original date when taken) or Pick a Date (to have all photos you're uploading have the same date).

10 To enter information about a specific picture, enter a description in the Say Something About This Photo box for that photo.

11 Click the Settings (gear) icon and select Change Date to enter when this photo was taken.

12 If you want to enter a location for a specific photo that's different from the location you set for the entire album, click the Settings icon and select Edit Location.

13 To tag a person in a given photo, click that person's face and enter his or her name when prompted.

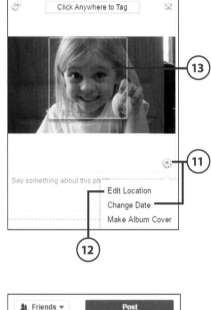

Photo Tagging

You identify people in your photos by *tagging* them—that is, you click a person in the photo, and then assign a friend's name to that part of the photo. You can then find photos where a given person appears by searching for that person's tag.

14 Click the Privacy button and make a selection—Public, Friends, Only Me, or Custom—to determine who can view the photos in this album.

15 Click the Post button.

Upload Photos to an Existing Photo Album

After you've created a photo album, you can easily upload more photos to that album.

(1) From your Photos page, click Albums to display your existing photo albums.

(2) Click the album to which you want to add new photos.

(3) When the album page opens, click + Add Photos to display the Open dialog box.

(4) Navigate to and select the photo(s) to upload.

(5) Click the Open button.

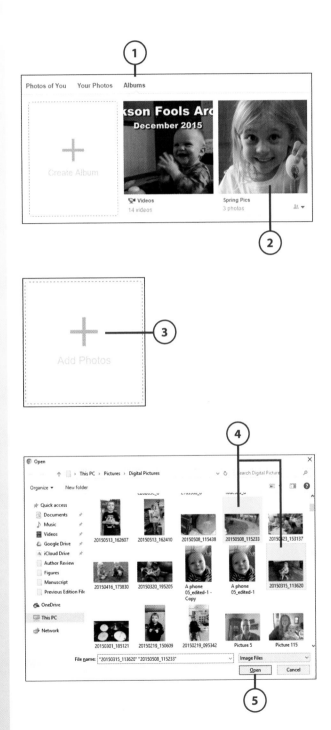

6 When the next page appears, you see the new photo(s) you've chosen to upload. Enter a description for each picture in the Say Something About This Photo box.

7 To change the default location or date, click the Settings icon and select either Edit Location or Change Date. (You can also click a person's face to tag that individual.)

8 Click the Post button. The new photos are now added to the existing album.

Delete a Photo

If you later discover that you've uploaded a photo you don't want to share, Facebook lets you delete individual photos within an album.

1 From the Facebook website, display the photo you want to delete, mouse over the photo to display the bottom menu, then click Options to display the pop-up menu.

2 Click Delete This Photo.

Click Confirm in the Delete
Photo panel.

Delete Photo ×

Are you sure you want to delete this photo?

Cancel **Confirm**

It's Not All Good

Deletion Is Final

When you delete a photo on Facebook, there's no way of undeleting that photo. You
can, however, re-upload the photo to the album from scratch.

When you delete a photo album, not only is the deletion final, but you also delete all
the photos within that album. Make sure you really want to delete a photo or album
before you proceed.

Delete a Photo Album

You're not limited to deleting single
photos. You can also delete complete
photo albums—and all the photos
within.

① Open the album you want to
delete, click the Settings button,
then select Delete Album.

② When prompted, click the
Delete Album button.

Delete Album? ×

Are you sure you want to delete Spring Pics? Photos in this album
will also be deleted.

Cancel **Delete Album**

>>>Go Further
POST A PHOTO SLIDESHOW

If you use an iPhone, the iOS Facebook app lets you post short slideshow videos based on photos taken or stored on your phone. (This feature presumably will also be available on Android phones at some point in the future—if not by the time you read this book.)

This new feature, dubbed Slideshow, automatically activates when you've posted five or more photos or videos within the past 24 hours. When you go to create a new post, Facebook suggests that you create a Slideshow. Select Yes, and Facebook fits your recently uploaded photos and videos into one of its Slideshow templates, which include transitions, movement, and background music. They're pretty neat, and you can share them with all your Facebook friends as a new status update.

Share a YouTube Video

In addition to uploading your own home videos, you can upload videos you find on YouTube (www.youtube.com), which is the world's largest online video community. Many Facebook users like to share videos they find on the YouTube site with their Facebook friends. Fortunately, both YouTube and Facebook make it easy to do this.

YouTube Account

To share YouTube videos, you first must have either a YouTube or Google account. Both are free.

1 From the YouTube site, navigate to the video you want to post to Facebook.

2 Click Share beneath the video player to expand the Share panel.

3 Click the Facebook icon to open the Post to Facebook window.

4 Enter an accompanying message into the Say Something About This box.

5 Click the Privacy button to determine who can view this video.

6 Click the Post to Facebook button. The video is posted as a status update to your Facebook timeline.

Linking Accounts

The first time you try to share a YouTube video on Facebook, you see the Facebook Login window. Enter your email address and Facebook password, and then click the Login button. (You won't see this window after the first time.)

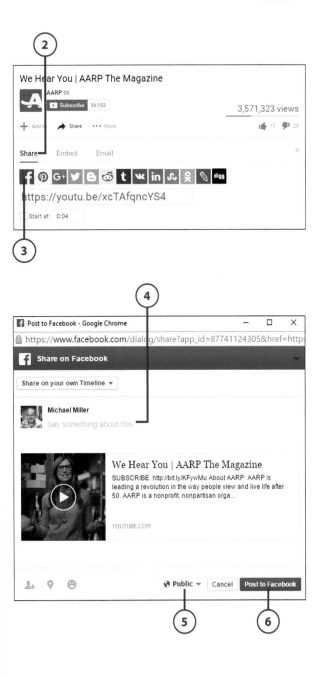

>>>*Go Further*

BROADCASTING LIVE VIDEO

Both the iOS and Android mobile apps let you share live video with your friends and others on Facebook. This video is streamed in real time as you shoot it; friends can "tune in" to see your live broadcast, or you can save the live video for others to view later. It's great for posting live from sporting events, birthday parties…you name it.

To broadcast live, tap the Publisher box to start a new post, and then tap Go Live. The front-facing (selfie) camera flies up, and you're prompted to describe your video. Tap to type a short description, and then tap Go Live.

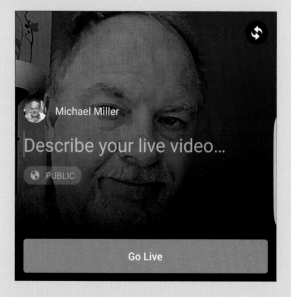

You're now streaming live video of yourself! Take this opportunity to greet your audience, and then tap the "reverse camera" icon to switch to the normal rear-facing camera. Aim your phone at whatever it is you're shooting, and stay live until you're finished. Tap the Finish button when you're done.

The video streams live to any interested friends, and then is saved and posted to your Timeline when you're done. It then shows up in all your friends' News Feeds, so they can watch your "live" broadcast after the fact—kind of like a Facebook rerun.

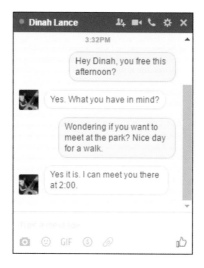

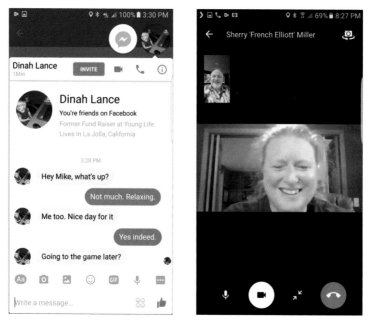

In this chapter, you find out how to send and receive private messages to and from other Facebook users.

→ Exchanging Text Messages on the Facebook Website
→ Mobile Messaging with the Messenger App
→ Video Chatting on Facebook

Chatting in Real Time—via Text or Video

Facebook is a public social network, which means it encourages public interaction between you and your friends. But you might not want all your communication to be public; sometimes you just want to send a private message to someone you know.

That's why, in addition to its public status updates, Facebook lets you send private messages to your Facebook friends. You can also use Facebook to conduct video chats, so you speak face-to-face with friends and family.

Exchanging Text Messages on the Facebook Website

Facebook lets any user send private text messages to any other user. These messages do not appear on either person's News Feed or Timeline page; it's the Facebook equivalent of private email.

If you're using Facebook on your computer, you can send and receive text messages on the Facebook website, using your web browser. (If you're using Facebook on your phone or tablet, skip to the "Mobile Messaging with the Messenger App" section, later in this chapter.)

Send a Text Message

Sending a private text message to another Facebook user is as easy as sending an email to that person—even easier, actually. Your master Facebook friends list functions much as a contacts list in an email program; you can add recipients to a message just by typing a few letters of their name.

(1) Click Messages in the toolbar.

(2) Click See All (at the bottom of the menu) to display the Messages page.

(3) Click the New Message button to display the New Message panel.

(4) Enter the name of the recipient into the To box.

(5) As you type, Facebook displays matching friends; select the desired recipient from the list.

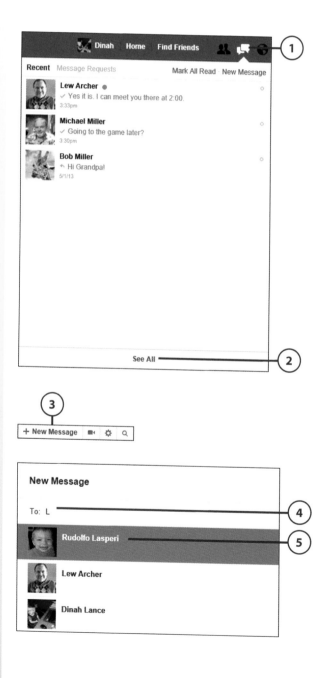

6 Enter your message into the Write a Message box.

7 Attach a photo to this message by clicking Add Photos and selecting the photo you want.

8 Press Enter or click the Send button to send the message on its way.

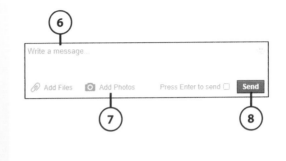

Read a Message

When you receive a new private message from a friend, you see a red number on top of the Messages icon on the Facebook toolbar. Click the Messages icon to read all your new private messages. Better yet, open the separate Messages page to view all your private messages—new and old.

1 Click the Messages button in the Facebook toolbar to view your most recent messages.

2 Click any message snippet to view the entire message in a separate message pane.

3 All your messages to and from this person are displayed in the form of a flowing conversation. The newest messages are at the bottom of the pane.

4 To respond to this person's latest message, enter your message into the bottom text box and press Enter.

Live Chat

If the person you're messaging is online at the same time you are, your private messages become a live text chat. Your friend sees your messages in real time, and you see her replies immediately, as well.

View All Messages

Clicking the Messages button on the toolbar only displays your most recent messages. You can view all messages you've received on the Messages page.

(1) On the Facebook toolbar, click the Messages button to display the menu of messages and options.

(2) Click See All at the bottom of the menu to open the Messages panel.

(3) All messages are listed in a scrolling list on the left side of the page. Click a message to view all messages to and from that person in the center section of the page.

(4) To reply to the current message, enter your text into the Write a Reply box at the bottom of the page, and then click the Reply button.

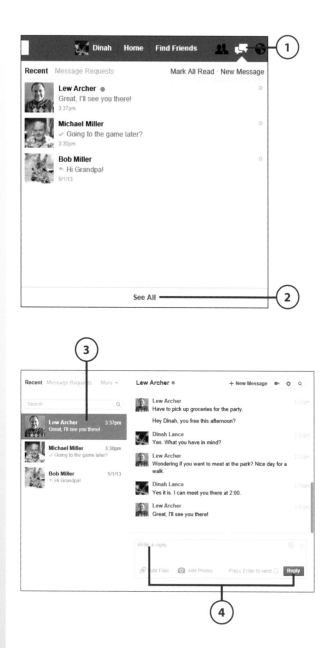

Mobile Messaging with the Messenger App

If you want to send and receive private text messages from your smartphone or tablet, you can't do it from the Facebook mobile app. Text/chat functionality has been removed from the app.

Instead, you need to use a separate app, called Facebook Messenger, to do this sort of instant messaging. Like the regular Facebook app, the Messenger app is free for downloading for both Apple and Android devices.

The Facebook Messenger app does more than just connect you with your Facebook friends, however. If you opt for the default installation, the Messenger app taps into your phone's contacts list and identifies those contacts who are also on Facebook. This means that you can instant message with any of your contacts who are also Facebook users, even if they're not currently on your friends list.

Note that the Messenger app looks a little different on Android devices than it does on your iPhone or iPad; in particular, the navigation icons are on the bottom in the iOS app, and on the top in the Android app. I'm showing the Android version of this app for the examples, but the same functionality exists on the iOS version.

Send and Receive Text Messages

Just like the Facebook website does, Messenger enables you to send and receive either real-time text messages or private email-like messages. If the person you want to talk to is online, you communicate in real-time text chat. If the person you want to talk to is not currently online, you send that person a private text message instead.

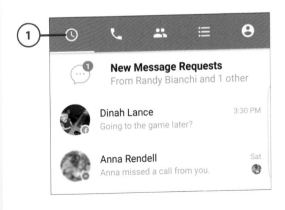

1 Tap the Recent or Home icon to view a list of your most recent text conversations and private messages.

2 Tap a conversation header to view messages between you and that person.

3 To continue the conversation, use your phone's onscreen keyboard to type a message into the Write a Message box.

4 Tap Send to send the message to the other person.

5 Create a new text message by tapping the Compose or + icon.

6 Tap Search (Android) or People (iOS) to display the People screen.

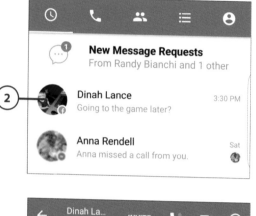

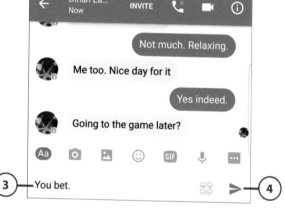

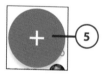

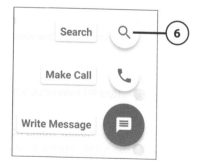

>>>*Go Further*

MESSAGING FROM THE CONTACTS SCREEN

You can also send messages directly from Messenger's Contacts screen. Tap the Contacts or People icon to display a list of your Facebook friends. Select the Messenger tab to view friends who have the Messenger app installed; select the Active tab to view friends who are currently online and available to chat. (Friends using Messenger have a blue Messenger icon next to their pictures; those who aren't have a gray Facebook icon instead.) Tap a person's name to start the conversation.

7 Your favorite contacts are listed on this screen. Tap a person's name or picture to begin the conversation, *or*...

8 Enter a person's name into the Search box at the top of the screen and then tap the person you want from the search results.

9 Enter your message into the Write a Message box.

10 Tap the Camera icon to take and send a photo.

11 Tap the Photos icon to send a photo stored in your phone's gallery.

12 Tap the Emoji icon to insert an emoji (emoticon—like a smiley face) in your message.

13 Tap Send to send the message.

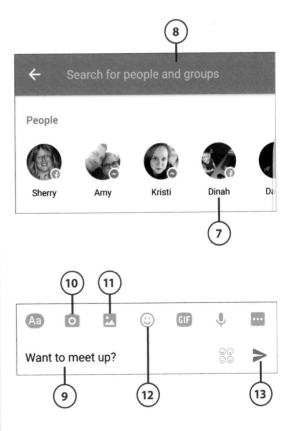

>>>Go Further
PHONE CALLS AND VIDEO CHATS

If the person you're messaging with is in your phone's contacts list, or if that person's phone number is listed with Facebook, you can turn your text message into a phone call. From within any conversation, tap the telephone icon to place the call.

You can also turn any text conversation into a video chat. From within any conversation, tap the Video Camera icon to begin a video chat.

Create a Group Conversation

The Messenger app isn't just for one-on-one conversations. You can also participate in group chats.

1. Tap the Groups icon to display the Groups page.

2. Any groups you've previously established are displayed here. Tap a group to open a new conversation with that group.

3. Tap the + button to create a new group.

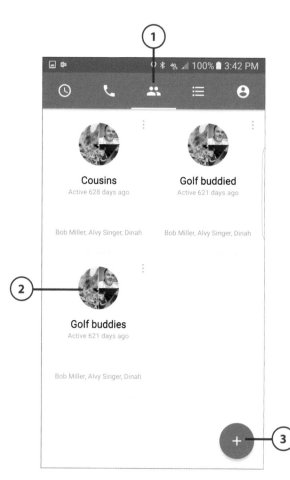

④ Tap Create Group.

⑤ Enter a name for your group.

⑥ Tap to select the names of people you want to include in this group.

⑦ Tap Create Group.

⑧ The new group now appears on the Groups page. Tap the group to open that group's conversation page.

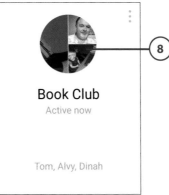

(9) Enter message text into the Type a Message box.

(10) Tap any of the other icons to send to the group a photo, emoji, voice message, or sticker.

(11) Tap Send to send the message. Your message and messages from other group members appear in the center of the screen.

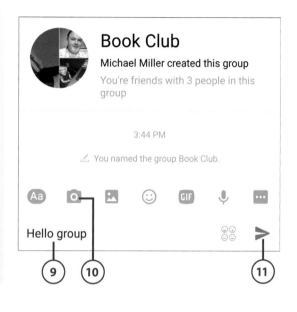

Video Chatting on Facebook

In addition to text messaging, Facebook also lets you talk to other Facebook users face-to-face via video chat. Video chatting is a great way to get up-close and personal with distant family and friends; you can see them and they can see you.

You can chat from your mobile phone or tablet, using the device's front-facing camera. You can also chat from a desktop or notebook computer, assuming it has a webcam built-in or attached.

Chat from the Messenger App

If you're connecting to Facebook from your mobile phone or tablet, you use the Messenger app to do your video chatting. You can chat with other phone and tablet users, or with users connecting to Facebook from their computers (assuming they have a webcam connected to their computer, of course).

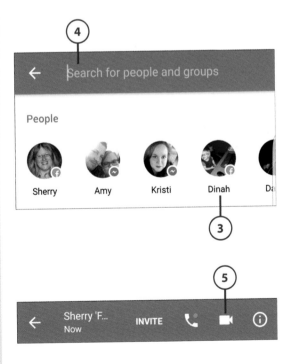

1. From within the Messenger app, tap the New Message (Android) or Compose (iOS) icon.

2. Tap Search (Android) or People (iOS) to display the People screen.

3. Tap a person's name or picture, or...

4. Enter a person's name into the Search (Android) or To (iOS) box and then tap the person you want from the search results.

5. Tap the Video icon at the top of the screen.

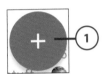

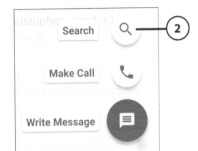

6 When your friend answers the call, you see her picture on your device's screen and the video chat begins. Your picture appears smaller in the upper-left corner.

7 Tap the red hang up button to end the video chat.

Video Chat from a Text Chat

You can also switch to a video chat from within a text chat. Just tap the Video icon at the top of the text chat screen and you'll open a video chat with the same person.

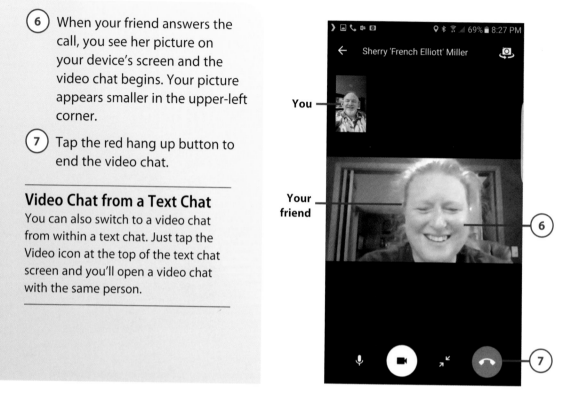

You

Your friend

Chat from the Facebook Website

You can also engage in video chats from your desktop or notebook computer. Most notebook computers have a built-in web camera (webcam); you may need to connect an external webcam to a desktop PC.

Install the Chat Applet

The first time you use Facebook's video chat, you are prompted to download and install the necessary background chat applet on your computer. (An applet is a small application that runs in the background—in this case, to enable video chat.) Follow the onscreen instructions to do so.

1. Click the Chat gadget at the bottom-right corner of any Facebook page to display the full Chat panel.

2. Click the name of the friend you want to chat with to open an individual Chat panel with the selected friend.

3. If your friend has a webcam and is available to chat, you'll see a camera icon at the top of the Chat panel. Click this Start a Video Call button to initiate the video chat.

4. When your friend answers the call, Facebook displays the video chat window. Your friend appears in the main part of the window; your picture is in a smaller window at the bottom right. All you have to do is talk.

5. When you're ready to close the chat, mouse over the chat window and then click the red End Call button.

Webcams and Microphones

Most webcams (whether attached or built in) also have built-in microphones. The camera in the webcam captures your picture, and the microphone in the webcam captures your voice. Just speak into the webcam to talk during a video chat.

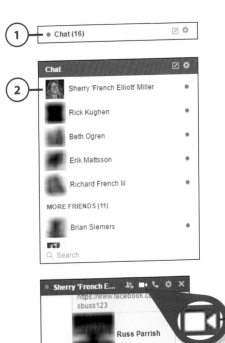

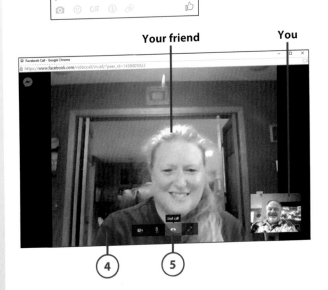

Your friend   You

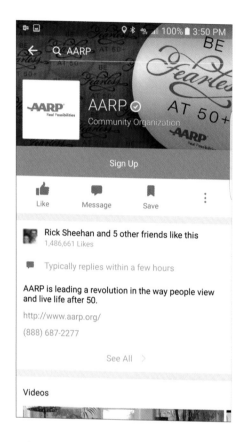

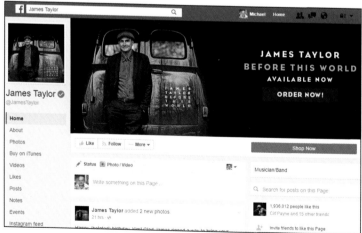

In this chapter, you find out how to follow companies and public figures on Facebook.

→ Finding and Following Companies and Public Figures
→ Managing the Pages You Follow

Liking Pages from Companies and Public Figures

Regular people on Facebook have their own Timeline pages. Businesses and public figures on Facebook, however, have their own special pages that are kind of like Timeline pages but different; they're tailored for the needs of customers and fans. These pages—rather unimaginatively called *Facebook Pages*—are how you keep abreast of what your favorite brands, products, and famous people are up to.

Finding and Following Companies and Public Figures

Even though businesses, celebrities, and public figures aren't regular users, they still want to use Facebook to connect with their customers and fans. They do this through Facebook pages—essentially Timeline pages for companies and public figures. If you're a fan of a given company or celebrity, you can "like" that entity's Facebook page—and keep abreast of what that company or individual is up to. It's kind of like joining an online fan club through Facebook.

Search for Companies and Public Figures

Many companies and organizations have Facebook pages for their brands and the products they sell. For example, you can find and follow pages for AARP, McDonalds, Starbucks, Walmart, and similar entities.

Many famous people—entertainers, athletes, news reporters, politicians, and the like—also have Facebook pages. So if you're a fan of Ellen DeGeneres, Jimmy Fallon, Sean Hannity, LeBron James, or James Taylor, you can follow any or all of them via their Facebook pages.

1 Enter one or more keywords that describe the person, company, or organization into the Search box. As you type, Facebook displays a list of pages and people that match your query.

2 If the page you want is listed, click it.

3 If the page you want is not listed, click See All Results to display a list of pages that match your query. Click the name of the page you want to view.

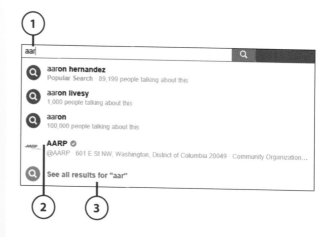

View and Like a Facebook Page

A professional Facebook page is very similar to a personal Timeline page, right down to the timeline of updates and activities. Pages can feature specialized content, however, which is located at the top of the page, under the cover image. For example, a musician's page might feature an audio player for that performer's songs; other pages might let you view pictures and videos, or even purchase items online.

Note that a celebrity or company on Facebook can't be your friend; that is, you can't add a professional page to your Facebook friends list. Instead, you can choose to like that page so that you can follow all the posts made by that entity. Unlike friending an individual, the pages you like do not follow all the status updates that you make on a regular basis.

Liking

Liking is a one-way thing. When you like a page you follow that page, but that page doesn't follow you.

---

1 Click the Like button to like (follow) this page.

2 Click About to read more about this person or company.

3 Click Photos to view the page's official pictures.

4 Click any other content to view that content.

5 Scroll down to view status updates and other postings.

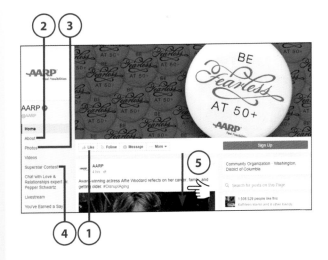

>>>Go Further

WHO GETS OR HAS A PAGE?

Just about any public person or entity can create a Facebook page. You can create Facebook pages for businesses, brands, and products; for musicians, actors, and other celebrities; for politicians, public servants, and other public figures; and for school classes, public organizations, special events, and social causes.

If you want to create your own page for your business or community organization, click the down arrow at the far right of the Facebook toolbar, select Create Pages, and follow the onscreen instructions from there. To create a page you must be an official representative of the group or company behind the page; fans can't create official pages for the companies and entertainers they follow.

View Page Posts in Your Pages Feed

Most companies and famous people on Facebook use their pages to keep their customers or fans informed of news and events. Some companies use their pages to offer promotions and special offers to customers.

Obviously, you can visit a given page to view the latest updates and content. You can also view updates from all the pages you like in Facebook's *pages feed*, which is kind of hidden in the navigation sidebar on the Facebook website. The pages feed is kind of like a News Feed for the pages you've liked, not for the individuals you're friends with.

1. On the Facebook website, click Home on the toolbar to display your Home page.

2. Scroll down the navigation sidebar to the Pages section and click Pages Feed to display the Pages feed in place of the normal News Feed.

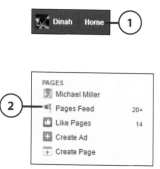

3 Posts from all the pages you follow are listed in the Pages feed, newest first. Scroll down to view more posts.

4 To return to the normal News Feed, click News Feed in the navigation sidebar or Home on the Facebook toolbar.

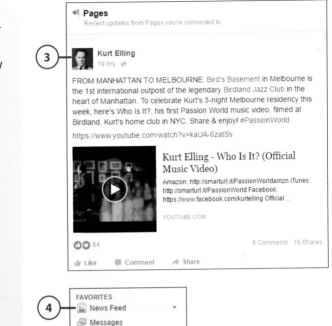

>>>Go Further
PROMOTED VERSUS ORGANIC POSTS

Facebook used to display all posts from those pages you like in your News Feed. It doesn't do that anymore. That's because Facebook is in the business of making money, and one way it does that is to charge companies to "promote" their page posts.

When a post is promoted (that is, paid for), Facebook displays it in the News Feeds of all of that page's followers. If a post is not promoted, Facebook probably won't display that post. If a company wants its followers to see its posts, it pretty much has to pay for that privilege.

Although some nonpromoted posts may show up in your News Feed from time to time, Facebook displays less than 20% of a page's "organic" (non-paid) posts. In other words, signing up to like a given page does not guarantee that you'll see all (or even most) of the posts to that page. If you want to see all that a company or person is posting, you have to go to that page to read the posts directly—or view your pages feed as described in the "View Page Posts in Your Pages Feed" section.

Managing the Pages You Follow

Some people only follow a handful of professional Facebook pages. Others find dozens of pages to follow. If you're a more prolific follower, you might want to manage your pages list over time.

View Your Favorite Pages

Not sure of whom exactly you're following? Then it's time to display all your favorite Facebook pages, in the pages list.

1. On the Facebook website, click your name in the toolbar to display your Timeline page.

2. Click More under your cover image and select Likes to display those pages you've liked.

3. Click the type of page you're looking for—Interests, Foods, Activities, and so on.

4. Click any given image to display that specific page.

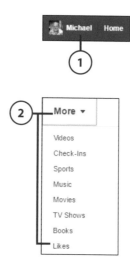

Unlike a Page

Just because you liked a given company or celebrity at one point in time doesn't mean you'll continue to like that entity forever. Your tastes change, after all, or you might find you don't like the posts a given page is making.

When you find yourself not liking a page so much, you can "unlike" that page. Unliking a page removes it from your Following feed, so you won't receive any more status updates or notifications from it.

While you can unlike a page from the page itself, it's often easier to view all the pages you've liked and do any unliking from there.

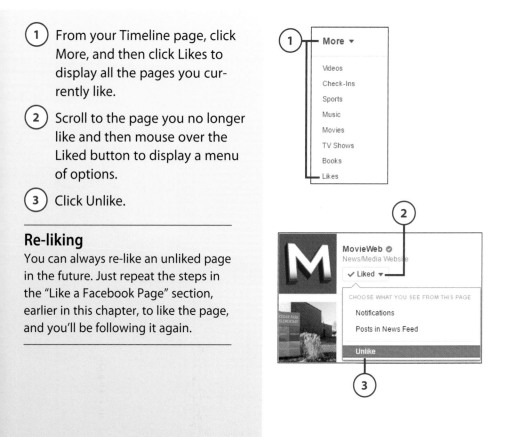

(1) From your Timeline page, click More, and then click Likes to display all the pages you currently like.

(2) Scroll to the page you no longer like and then mouse over the Liked button to display a menu of options.

(3) Click Unlike.

Re-liking

You can always re-like an unliked page in the future. Just repeat the steps in the "Like a Facebook Page" section, earlier in this chapter, to like the page, and you'll be following it again.

→ Finding and Joining Facebook Groups
→ Participating in Facebook Groups
→ Using Groups to Reconnect with Old Friends

Participating in Interesting Facebook Groups

As you read in the previous chapter, Facebook Pages are like fan clubs for companies and celebrities and other public figures. There are other kinds of "clubs" on Facebook, however, in the form of public *groups*. Facebook has groups for all types of interests.

Many of you are probably interested in groups that reunite you with people you've known in the past. These could be groups devoted to your old town or neighborhood, your old grade school or high school, or even activities you used to participate in. These groups are great ways to reminisce about the old times and keep in touch with people you knew back then.

Finding and Joining Facebook Groups

If you want to make new friends—and reconnect with old ones—one of the best ways to do so is to search out others who share your interests.

If you're into gardening, look for gardeners. If you're into recreational vehicles, look for fellow RVers. If you're a wine lover, look for other connoisseurs of the grape.

Even better, look for people who've shared your life experiences. That means connecting with people who went to the same schools, lived in the same neighborhoods, and participated in the same activities.

You can find people who share your history and hobbies in Facebook *groups*. A group takes the form of a special Facebook page, a place for people interested in that topic to meet online and exchange information and pleasantries.

Search for Groups

Facebook offers tens of thousands of different groups online, so chances are you can find one or more that suit you. The key is finding a particular group that matches what you're interested in—which you do by searching.

(1) Go to the Facebook search box (on either the website or on the mobile app) and enter one or more keywords that describe what you're looking for. For example, if you're interested in sewing, enter **sewing**. If you're looking for a group for graduates from your old high school, enter **high school name alumni**. (Replace *high school name* with the name of your high school, of course.) If you want to find a group created by people who live on the west side of Indianapolis, enter **Indianapolis west side**.

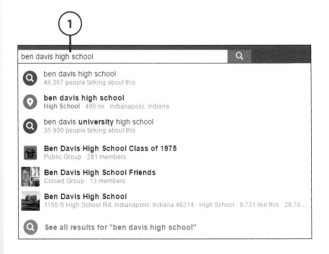

2 As you type, Facebook displays a list of items that match your query. To view a group's Facebook page, click the name of the group.

3 If you don't see any matching groups in this short list, click See All Results to display more groups that match your query.

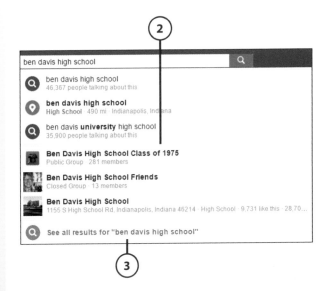

Browse for Groups

There are also several ways to browse for Facebook groups—by following Facebook's suggestions, exploring groups that your friends belong to, and viewing groups for your local area.

1 On the Home page of Facebook's website, scroll down the navigation sidebar to the Groups section and click Discover Groups. This displays the Groups page.

2 By default, the Discover tab is selected. This page displays a number of groups in which Facebook thinks you might be interested. Click a thumbnail at the top to view groups in that category.

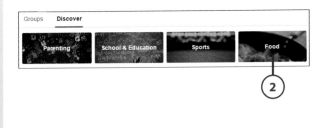

3 Go to the Friends section to view groups that your Facebook friends have joined. Click any group name to visit that group's page, or click See All to see more of these groups.

4 Go to the Local section to view groups located in your area, such as those for local schools, organizations, and towns. Click any group name to visit that group's page, or click See All to see more of these groups.

5 Scroll to other sections on this page to view more groups within selected categories.

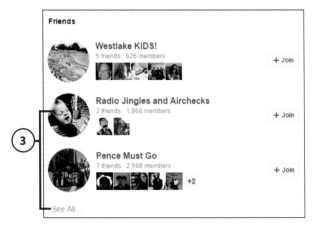

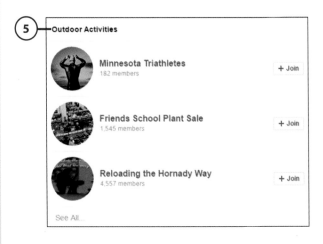

Join a Group

After you find a group, you can officially join it—and then participate to whatever degree suits your fancy. You can join a group from the search results page, or from the group's Facebook page.

1. To join a group from the Groups page or any search results page, click the Join button.

2. To join a group from its Facebook page, click Join Group.

>>>Go Further
PUBLIC AND CLOSED GROUPS

Most groups are classified as Public groups, meaning they're open for all Facebook members to join. Some groups, however, are Closed groups, which require that the group administrator approve all requests for membership.

To join a Closed group, you must apply for membership, and hope that your request is granted. When you click the Join button, a request goes to the group administrator. If your request is granted, you receive a message that you've been approved and are now an official member of the group. If your request is not granted, you don't get any response.

Participating in Facebook Groups

What can you do in a Facebook group? A lot, actually. You can read the latest news, discover new information, view photos and movies, exchange messages with other group members, and engage in online discussions about the topic at hand. It's just like participating in a real-world club, except you do it all on Facebook.

Visit a Group Page

Although you can view a feed of messages from all your groups (covered later in this chapter), most people prefer to visit individual group pages. This enables you to partake in all of the resources available in a given group.

1. In the Facebook mobile app, tap the More button then scroll to the Groups section. In the Android app, tap See All to view all the groups you like, *or…*

2. On the Facebook website, scroll down the navigation sidebar to the Groups section and click More. This displays the Groups page with the Groups tab selected.

3. Scroll down to the Your Groups section and click the name of a group to open its Facebook page.

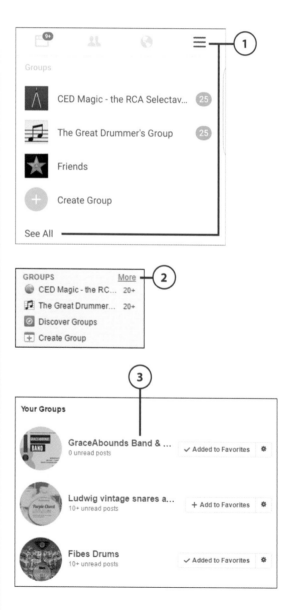

Read and Reply to Posts

After you open a group page, you can read posts from other members of the group and then like and comment on those posts as you would normal Facebook status updates.

Group Posts

Posts that you make on a group's Facebook page may be displayed only on that page, not in individual members' News Feeds, depending on their Facebook settings.

1. Open the group's page and view all posts from members in the scrolling feed in the middle of the page.

2. Click Like to like a particular post.

3. Click Comment to reply to a post and then enter your reply into the Comment box.

4. Click Share to share a post with your Facebook friends in your Facebook feed.

Anna Rendell
May 10 at 10:22pm

Thanks for a fun rehearsal, all! I posted a live video from practice over on the new GraceAbounds FB page - take a peek ☺
http://facebook.com/thegraceaboundsband

See many of you tomorrow!

GraceAbounds
Musician/Band
34 likes

Save

👍 Like   💬 Comment   ➤ Share

Herb Dixon and Erik Chrissis   ✓ Seen by 18

Write a comment...

Create a New Post

Not only can you reply to posts made by other members, you can start a new discussion by creating a new post on the group's page. Other group members can then like and reply to your message.

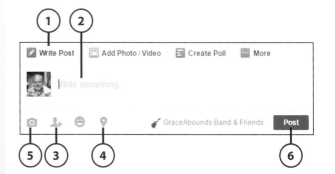

(1) Open the group's page, scroll to the Publisher box, and click Write Post.

(2) Enter your post into the Write Something box; this expands the box.

(3) Click the Tag People in Your Post button to tag another friend in this post.

(4) Click the Check In button to add a location to this post.

(5) Click the Add Photos or a Video (camera) button to add photographs or a video to this post.

(6) Click the Post button to post your message to the group.

View Group Members

Who belongs to this particular group? It's easy to view all the members of a Facebook group.

1. Open the group's page and click Members to display a list of group members.

2. Search for a particular member by entering that person's name into the Find a Member box and pressing Enter.

3. Click a member's name to view that person's Timeline page.

4. Mouse over a member's name to view more information about that person.

5. Click Add Friend to add that group member as a friend.

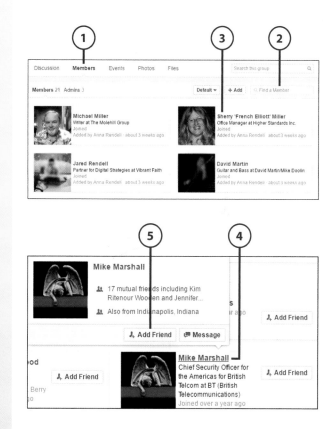

View Group Photos

Most groups let members post photos (and, in some cases, videos) of interest to other group members. If you're a member of a crafts group, for example, members might post photos of projects they've created. If you're a member of a group of old high school friends, members might post old photos from your school days. Viewing group photos, then, can be a fun activity.

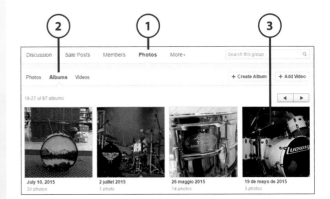

1. Open the group's page and click Photos to display a list of group photos and photo albums.

2. Click Albums to view all photo albums in the group.

3. Click a photo album to view all the photos in that album.

Get Notified of Group Activity

If you're active in a Facebook group, you might want to be notified when others post to the group. You can opt to receive notifications of each post made, or only of those posts made by your friends.

1. Open the group's page and click Notifications.

(2) Select All Posts to receive a notification whenever a post is made to the group.

(3) Select Highlights to receive notification of only friends posts and other important posts.

(4) Select Friends' Posts to receive a notification whenever one of your Facebook friends posts to this group.

(5) Select Off to not receive any notifications from this group.

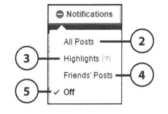

Leave a Group

If you grow tired of irrelevant or uninteresting posts in a given group, you can choose to unsubscribe from or leave a group.

(1) From the group's page, mouse over the Joined button.

(2) Click Leave Group to permanently leave the group.

(3) Click Unfollow Group to stay in the group but not see group posts in your News Feed.

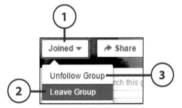

Using Groups to Reconnect with Old Friends

On the surface, it's easy to think of Facebook groups as 21st-century versions of the homeroom clubs you had back in high school. You know: chess club, knitting club, model airplane club, and the like.

Although there certainly are a huge number of these club-like Facebook groups, there are also groups that are more about times and places than they are about hobbies and interests. As such, these groups attempt to reconnect people with shared experiences.

I belong to a number of groups that connect me back to the days of my youth. For example, I grew up on the west side of Indianapolis, and now I belong to a Facebook group called Growing Up on Indy's Westside. It's a fun little group, with people posting faded pictures of old haunts, and lots of discussions about the way things used to be and what we used to do back then. I can't say I contribute too often, but it's always fun to read what others post.

I also belong to a "Where is and/or who do you remember?" group for my high school. This is a great place to find out what my old classmates have been up to in the decades since graduation, and it has lots of posts asking about individual students, teachers, and events. It's a nice stroll down memory lane.

The point is, participating in Facebook groups can be a great way to reconnect with your past. You might even meet up with some of your old friends in these groups, or make some new friends you should have made way back then. It's kind of a virtual blast from the past, and we have the Facebook social network to thank for it.

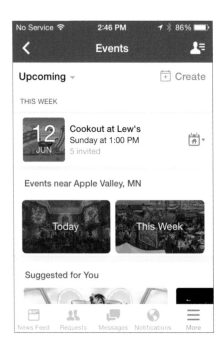

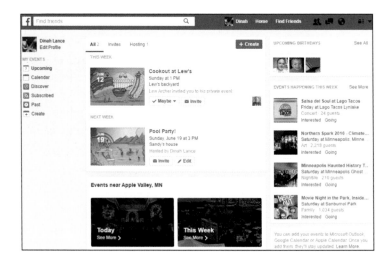

In this chapter, you find out how to respond to event notifications and schedule your own events on Facebook—as well as celebrate your friends' birthdays online.

→ Dealing with Invitations to Events
→ Scheduling a New Event
→ Celebrating Birthdays

14

Attending Events and Celebrating Birthdays

Facebook lets you do more than just post and read status updates to and from your friends and family. You can also use Facebook as a kind of event scheduler, so you can manage parties, meetings, reunions, and the like from within Facebook.

The most common type of event is a birthday, and Facebook helps out there, too. Facebook notifies you of your friends' and family members' upcoming birthdays and makes it easy for you to send your birthday greetings. Facebook even announces your birthday to your friends—so sit back and wait for those well wishes to arrive!

Dealing with Invitations to Events

You use Facebook to keep in touch with all your friends and family, so it's only natural to use Facebook to schedule events that might involve these same people. You're all online and on Facebook, after all; why not use Facebook to notify people of upcoming events?

Facebook's events feature lets you do just that—schedule events and invite your Facebook friends to those events, using Facebook's built-in messaging system. In effect, Facebook creates a new page for each event scheduled, and whoever creates the event can then invite people to view the page and attend the event. If you receive an invitation to a Facebook event, you can then decide to accept or decline the invitation.

Respond to an Event Invitation

When you've been invited to an event, you receive a notification about the event. Click the notification to view the Facebook page for that event and then let the host know whether you'll be attending.

No Obligation
You should feel no obligation to accept any specific event. Only accept those you genuinely want to and can attend.

1. Click or tap the Notifications icon to see recent event invitations.

2. Click or tap the event notification to display the event page.

③ Click or tap Going to accept the invitation.

④ Click or tap Maybe if you're not sure whether you'll attend.

⑤ Click or tap Can't Go if you don't want to accept the invitation.

View an Event Page

When a friend schedules a new event, Facebook creates a page for that event. You can view the event page to learn more about the event.

① From the Facebook website, go to your Home page and click Events in the navigation sidebar to display the Events page.

② In the Facebook mobile app, tap More and then tap Events to display the Events page.

3 In the iOS app, tap the down arrow next to Upcoming and select one of the following: Upcoming (all upcoming events to which you've been invited), Invites (any pending invitations), Saved (events you've saved), Hosting (events you've created and are hosting), and Past (events that have already taken place).

4 In the Android app, scroll along the top to select from the following: Upcoming, Invites, Saved, Birthdays (friends with upcoming birthdays), Hosting, and Past Events.

5 On the Facebook website, click to select from the following: All, Invites, and Hosting.

6 Click or tap the name of an event to view the page for that event.

7 Click or tap the appropriate option to tell the host whether or not you're going to this event.

8 View information about the event, such as the date, time, and location.

9 Click or tap Show Map to view a map of the event's location. (If this link isn't visible, the host hasn't entered an exact address for the event.)

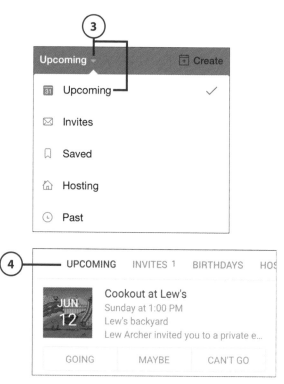

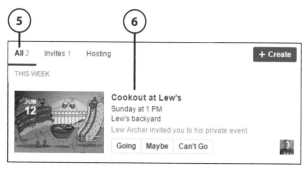

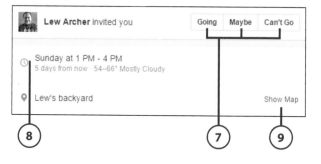

10 See who's attending the event by clicking Going in the Guests pane.

11 To see who may be going (but aren't fully committed), click Maybe in the Guests box.

12 To see who has been invited but hasn't yet responded, click Invited in the Guests box.

13 View messages about this event in the feed beneath the information box.

14 Use the Publisher box to post your own messages to the people invited to this event.

>>>Go Further
FACEBOOK EVENTS

What exactly is an event? On Facebook, an event is any item on your personal schedule. Events can be small and private, such as a doctor's appointment or dinner with a friend. Events can also be large and public, such as a community meeting or family reunion.

This means that you can use Facebook events to invite friends to backyard BBQs, block parties, golf dates, and card games. You can also use Facebook events to invite family members to birthday parties, holiday gatherings, and family reunions.

The events you create don't have to be real-world, physical events, either. You can schedule virtual events, such as inviting all your friends to watch a specific TV show or sporting event on a given evening. You can also schedule online events, such as seminars and conferences on sites that offer such options. In other words, you don't have to meet someone in person to share an event with them. It's all part of the social networking thing.

Scheduling a New Event

You don't have to wait to be invited to an event. You can also schedule your own Facebook events.

Maybe your neighborhood association has a meeting coming up. Maybe you're hosting a house party for some friends. Or maybe you just want to let everyone know about an upcoming anniversary. Whatever the case, Facebook makes it relatively easy to create new events and invite some or all of your Facebook friends to these events.

Create an Event

Facebook lets you create all manner of events, from parties to community meetings, and invite selected friends to those events. You can then manage that event through the event's Facebook page.

We'll examine how to create an event from the Facebook website. The process is similar with the mobile app.

1. From Facebook's Home page, click Events in the navigation sidebar to display your Events page.

2. Click the Create button to display the Create New Event panel.

3. By default, Facebook events are private—visible only to those who receive invitations. To make this a public event, click the Create Private Event button and select instead Create Public Event.

4 Add a photo for this event by clicking Upload Photo and selecting the picture you want to use.

5 Select a visual theme for this event page by clicking Choose a Theme and making a selection. (You can choose either a theme or use a photo, but you can't do both.)

6 Enter the name of the event into the Event Name box.

7 Specify the event's location by entering the location into the Location box.

Location

You can enter an exact address as the event's location, a city or state, or even just "My House" or "Room 223 in the Henry Building."

8 Click the date control and select a date from the pop-up calendar.

9 Enter the start time of the event into the Time box.

10 If you entered a start time you can also enter an end time for the event. Click the End Time link to display the End section, and then use the controls to set the end date and time.

✉ Create Private Event ▾   ✕

You're creating a private event. To protect the privacy of guests you won't be able to change it to public later.

Event Photo	⊙ Upload Photo	▣ Choose a Theme
Event Name	Add a short, clear name	
Location	Include a place or address	
Date/Time	6/7/2016 📅 6:00 PM ◷ CDT	+ End Time
Description	Tell people more about the event	

✓ Guests can invite friends

Cancel   **Create**

(11) Enter any additional details about the event into the Description box.

(12) Click the Create button to create the event.

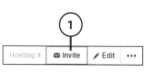

Invite Friends to Your Event

Once you've created an event, you need to invite people to attend that event. You do this from the newly created event page.

(1) From the event page, click the Invite button to display the Invite pane.

(2) Check those friends you want to invite.

(3) Click the Send Invites button to send out the desired invitations.

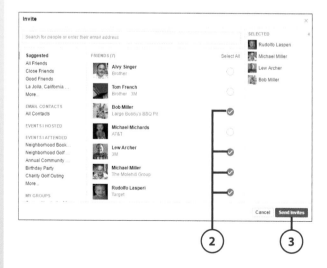

Edit or Cancel an Event

It happens. Even the best-laid plans go astray, and you may be forced to change your plans, or even cancel a planned event. Here's how you do it.

1. Open the event page and click the Edit button to display the Edit Event panel.

2. Click to edit any specific piece of information about the event.

3. Cancel the event by clicking Cancel Event.

4. When prompted, make sure Cancel Event is selected.

5. Enter a new post to let people know why the event was cancelled.

6. Click Confirm.

Hosting ⬦   ✉ Invite   ✏ Edit   •••

Edit Event   ✕

Event Photo

Drag to Reposition

Event Name   Pool Party!

Location   Sandy's house

Start   6/19/2016   3:00PM   CDT

End   6/19/2016   6:00PM   CDT   Remove

Description   We're having a big pool party at Sandy's house! Bring your swimsuits and pool toys -- kids and spouses welcome, too.

Cancel Event   Cancel Save

What do you want to do?   ✕

• **Cancel Event**
Guests will be notified that this event was canceled. You won't be able to modify the event, but people will still be able to post.

Delete Event
Guests will be notified that this event was canceled and everything posted to the event will be deleted.

Add a post to the event with more info:

Cancel **Confirm**

Celebrating Birthdays

Facebook knows a lot about you and your friends, including when you were born. To that end, Facebook does a nice social service by letting you know when someone's birthday is approaching—so that you can send your birthday wishes.

Personal Replies

Most people receive a lot of Facebook greetings on their birthdays. Don't be disappointed if you don't receive a personal thank you from the birthday baby.

View Upcoming Birthdays

Facebook notifies you when it's one of your friends' birthday. You can then leave that person a happy birthday message. It's what people do on Facebook!

1 In the iOS mobile app, tap the More icon, tap Events to display the Events page, and then scroll down to the Upcoming Birthdays section.

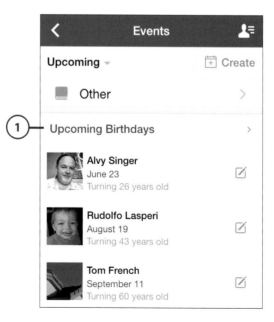

(2) In the Android mobile app, tap the More icon, tap Events to display the Events page, and then tap the Birthdays tab.

(3) On the Facebook website, upcoming birthdays are displayed in the upper-right corner of the Home page. Click within the notification box to display all upcoming birthdays. *Or…*

(4) Tap a friend's name or picture to view the friend's Timeline page.

(5) Enter a birthday message into the text box and then click Post.

(6) Click or tap See Upcoming Birthdays to view other birthdays.

Public Only

Facebook only notifies you of birthdays from friends who have opted to make their birthdates public. Friends with private birthdays do not appear in the birthday list.

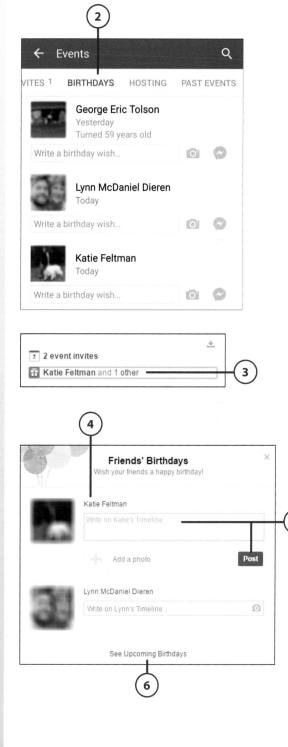

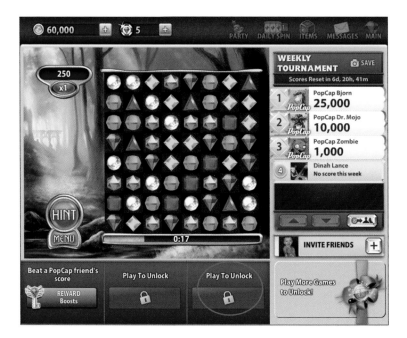

In this chapter, you find out how to have more fun on Facebook with social games.

→ Discovering Facebook Games
→ Managing and Deleting Facebook Games

Playing Games

Millions of Facebook users of every age are going online to play games—either by themselves or with their Facebook friends. What kinds of games are available on Facebook? Read on to find out!

Discovering Facebook Games

Facebook offers a variety of fun and often addictive games for its users to play. These games, sometimes called *social games* (because you get to share scores and other game info with your friends), are played on the Facebook site itself, after you're logged in. Some of these are single-player games that you play yourself (versus the computer) or multi-player games that you play against your friends and other Facebook users. Some of these games have millions of players on Facebook!

You can find Facebook games in a variety of categories, including

- Action games
- Adventure games
- Arcade games
- Bingo games
- Board games
- Builder games
- Card games
- Card battle games
- Match 3 games
- Poker and table games

- Puzzle games
- Role playing games
- Runner games
- Simulation games
- Slot games
- Sports games
- Strategy games
- Trivia games
- Word games

Third-Party Games

Most of the social games you find on Facebook are created by third-party application developers, not by Facebook itself. The vast majority of these games are available free of charge.

Find Games on the Facebook Website

When you want to play games on your computer, the Game Center on Facebook's website is the place to go. You can browse the Game Center by category to find what you're looking for, or you can search for specific games.

1 On the Facebook website, open the Home page, scroll down the navigation sidebar until you reach the Apps section, and then click Games.

(2) This displays the Game Center page. Make sure the Find Games tab is selected.

(3) The Home tab, underneath the Find Games tab, displays recommended and popular games in a variety of categories. Scroll down the page to view more games in more categories.

(4) Click the Top Charts tab to view categories of the most popular games on Facebook, such as Most Popular, Popular Among Friends, and Top Grossing.

(5) Click the Casual tab header to view games in the Puzzle, Board Game, Simulation, Match 3, Runner, Cards, Builder, and Trivia & Word categories.

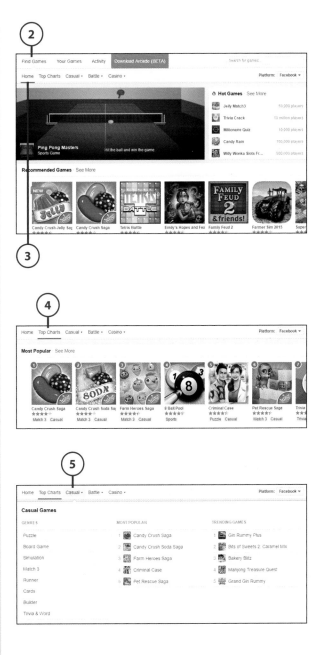

6 Click the Battle tab header to view games in the Action, Role Playing, Strategy, Card Battle, and Sports categories.

7 Click the Casino tab header to view games in the Slots, Poker & Table, and Bingo categories.

8 To search for a specific game, enter the name of the game into the search box at the top-right corner of the page. Matching games display as you type.

9 Click the name of a game to view that item's Facebook page—and start playing!

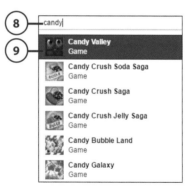

Play a Facebook Game

Playing a game on Facebook is pretty much like playing any other game on your computer. Here's how to start playing a game:

1 From the Game Center, click the name of the game to open its Facebook page.

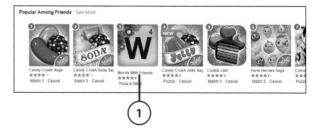

(2) Click the Play Now button to begin playing the game.

>>>Go Further

GAMES IN THE FACEBOOK MOBILE APP

The whole issue of Facebook games is a little different when you're using Facebook's mobile app. In fact, the mobile app really doesn't have any game functionality built in. Instead, when you install a game from the mobile app, you're just installing regular game apps from either Apple's App Store (for iOS devices) or the Google Play Store (for Android devices).

In either case, you can find suggested games on your mobile device by tapping the More button and scrolling to and tapping Games (on an Android device) or Apps and then Games (on an iPhone or iPad). Click a game to go to its page in the respective app store and then download it. To play a game, tap the game's icon on your device's home screen.

Managing and Deleting Facebook Games

Over time you may find that you're playing certain games less and less—if at all. You can manage all the games you're playing from Facebook's Game Center, and delete those you no longer play.

1. On Facebook's Home page, scroll down the navigation sidebar until you reach the Apps section, and click Games to display the Game Center.

2. Click the Your Games tab to view those games you've installed.

3. Click the gear button for the game you want to manage or delete; this displays a management panel for that game.

4. To change who can see that you're playing this game, click the App Visibility button and select from these options: Public, Friends, Friends of Friends, Only Me, or Custom.

5. To select whether or not the game can send you notifications, scroll down and click the Send You Notifications button and select either Yes or No.

6 To delete the game, click the Remove App link at the bottom of the panel.

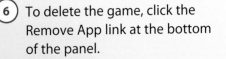

App Terms · App Privacy Policy · Remove App · Report App

6

7 When prompted to confirm the removal, click the Remove button.

Remove Words With Friends?

This will remove the app from your account, your bookmarks and the list of apps you use (found in your settings). Learn more.

Note: Words With Friends may still have the data you shared with them. For details about removing this data, please contact Words With Friends or visit the Words With Friends Privacy Policy.

☑ Delete all your Words With Friends activities including posts, photos and videos on Facebook. This may take a few minutes.

Cancel   **Remove**

7

It's Not All Good

Social Games and Privacy

Many Facebook games are social in nature, in that they use your Facebook friends list to either obtain information about your friends or send information to them regarding your activity within the game. That's both good and bad.

One of the good things about a social game is that it helps to create a larger community of users by linking you with your friends. The game might also use your friends' information to provide additional benefit to you. (For example, a game might request that your friends send you in-game items or points.)

The bad thing about a social game is that it makes a lot of personal information public. When you agree to share your information (including your friends list) with the game, you're relinquishing some degree of privacy. You're also betraying the trust of your friends by letting the game access some of their personal information, or post annoying information to their News Feeds. You might be comfortable doing that, and that's fine. But some users don't want to make everything public, and especially don't want to breach their friends' privacy. If that's how you think, then don't sign up for social games that request you share this information. If you don't join in, you won't be jeopardizing your privacy.

Tom French
1 min ·

Look who got a first-place ribbon at the state science fair! Great going, Collin!

👍 Like   💬 Comment   ➤ Share

Write a comment...
Press Enter to post.

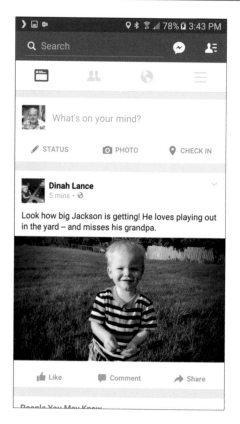

🔍 Search

What's on your mind?

✏️ STATUS   📷 PHOTO   📍 CHECK IN

Dinah Lance
5 mins ·

Look how big Jackson is getting! He loves playing out in the yard -- and misses his grandpa.

👍 Like   💬 Comment   ➤ Share

People You May Know

In this chapter, you discover the best ways to use Facebook to get closer to the youngest members of your family.

→ Are Kids Still Using Facebook?
→ How to Connect with Younger Users on Facebook
→ Five Things *Not* to Do with Your Kids and Grandkids on Facebook

Keeping in Touch with Your Kids and Grandkids on Facebook

Facebook is very popular among middle-aged and older users today, but it started out as a social network for college students. While the current generation of college students has moved onto newer, hipper social media for their own personal use, most younger users still maintain a presence on Facebook—primarily to keep in touch with the older members of their families.

Are Kids Still Using Facebook?

Facebook might be new to you, but it's old news for most younger users. In fact, Facebook used to be the place where all the cool kids hung out. That was probably before you signed up, however. Today, Facebook's user base has shifted toward the older side, and younger users are either using Facebook less or abandoning it completely.

Let's face it—if you're a kid, you don't want to do much of anything that your parents and grandparents are also doing. A website or social network just isn't cool if all the older people you know are using it, too.

And older users definitely are using Facebook. The fastest growing age group on Facebook today is users aged 55 and up, whereas users 35 and up now represent almost half of Facebook's user base. This means that kids in their teens and twenties make up less than half of all Facebook users—even though they used to rule the roost.

This demographic shift is due in part to more older people joining up, but also to equally large numbers of younger users leaving. From 2011 to 2014, Facebook lost more than 3 million users aged 13 to 17, and another 3 million in the 18 to 24 age group. Like it or not, Facebook is definitely becoming a hangout for older users.

Before this shift, Facebook used to be a good place for parents and grandparents to connect with their kids and grandkids. That's less true today, although there's still a place for Facebook in the intergenerational communication chain.

Even though a lot of younger users are leaving Facebook for good, even more are remaining on Facebook but just using it less. Instead of checking in constantly throughout the day, today's younger generation of Facebook users are more likely to check in just once a day, or maybe once every few days.

In other words, your grandkids and their friends are maintaining their ties to the Facebook community, even as they explore new social networking opportunities elsewhere. Why stay on Facebook if it's no longer cool? Simple: To stay in touch with those non-cool older family members.

That's right—younger users recognize Facebook's valuable role in connecting all family members—younger and older. Your kids, grandkids, and nephews and nieces are staying on Facebook *because* you're there—not in spite of it. They know that you use Facebook to share family news and photos, and there's value in that. It's easier for them to keep up with what's going on by checking in on Facebook every few days. The younger generation might not be using Facebook to talk to one another as much anymore, but they're using it to talk to you and other people who are important to them.

Knowing this changes the way you might have otherwise used Facebook to connect with your grandkids. You no longer have to sneak around the dark corners of Facebook to keep tabs on what the kids are doing; instead, they expect you to be right up front with your comments and pictures and such.

How to Connect with Younger Users on Facebook

If you're in your sixties, your thirty-something and forty-something children are likely long-time Facebook users. They know how to use Facebook to share and connect with friends and family, and expect you to either do the same or learn how. You'll find them checking their Facebook feeds several times a day.

Your teenage and twenty-something children and grandchildren are also expert in using Facebook, but they use it a whole lot less. They check their News Feeds no more than a few times each week, primarily to see what their parents and other family members are up to. Some still use Facebook to keep in touch with distant friends, although this is becoming less common. Like their parents, these kids are savvy Facebook users, even if they're not on all the time.

Knowing this, you need to connect with your children and grandchildren at a similar level of expertise. You need to know not only how to connect via Facebook, but also what is best to share in that environment. Let's walk through what you need to do.

Make Friends with Your Kids and Grandkids

The first step in using Facebook to connect with your younger family members is to add them to your friends list. It shouldn't be too hard to find your children, grandchildren, nieces, and nephews on Facebook, and then send out the necessary friend requests. When your family members are on your friends list, every post they make should show up in your News Feed.

It's Not All Good

Selected Posts

By default, your kids' and grandkids' posts are visible to all their Facebook friends, including you. More tech-savvy youngsters, however, might figure out how to fine-tune their privacy settings and exclude you (and other family members) from some or all of their posts. This means you *don't* see everything they post in your News Feed. There's no way around this.

1 Facebook might suggest your family members as friends when you first sign up or when you click the Friend Requests button on the toolbar—especially if you have their addresses in your email contacts list. If so, click the Add Friend button.

Finding Friends

Learn how to find family and friends on Facebook in Chapter 3, "Finding Friends on Facebook."

2 Alternatively, you can do a simple search for your kids and grandkids on the Facebook site. Use the search box in the Facebook toolbar to search for **people named *john doe*** and your family member's name should pop up. (In this and other examples, replace "john doe" with the name of the person you're searching for.)

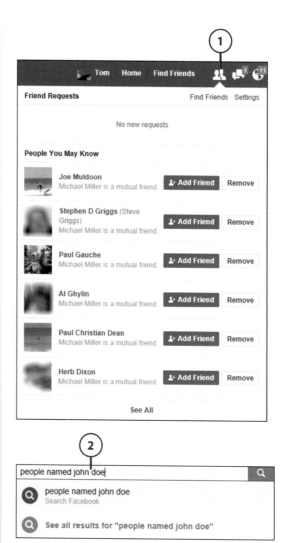

Put Your Family Members in a Special Friends List

Just as you can read your kids' and grandkids' posts on Facebook, they can also read your status updates in their News Feeds. However, your grandkids might not be interested in everything you post, especially those posts that deal with issues of interest to you and your friends.

The solution is to not send all your posts to the youngsters. Instead, you can create a *friends list* that contains only selected family members. You can then opt to hide your posts from members of that list—or send selected posts only to your family members. It's an easy way to deal with groups of people (in this instance, your family members) with a single click.

It's Not All Good

They Love You, But...

Depending on what you post on Facebook, your kids and grandkids might find your status updates charming. Or they might find them embarrassing or even totally uninteresting. Let's face it: The kinds of things that interest someone our age aren't likely to be engrossing to the average teenager. For that matter, all those words of wisdom and inspiration that you like to post are likely to be roundly ignored by youngsters with more immediate things on their minds.

In other words, don't expect the younger generations to like and comment on everything you post. At best, they might read your posts and then move on. At worst, they might figure out how to block your posts—or even unfriend you.

1. Start by creating a new Facebook friends list that contains all your children and grandchildren. Go to the Timeline page for your first family member, click the Friends button, and then click Add to Another List.

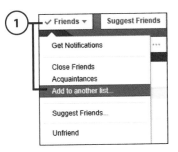

(2) Facebook creates a number of "smart" lists, based on personal information you've added to your account. One of these smart lists, named Family, is just for your family members. Click Family to add this person to your Family list.

(3) For each of your other family members, go to his or her Time-line page, click the Friends but-ton, and add him or her to your Family list.

(4) Now you can configure your pri-vacy settings so that your family members don't see the bulk of your posts. Click Privacy Short-cuts on the Facebook toolbar, select Who Can See My Stuff?, and then go to the Who Can See My Future Posts? section.

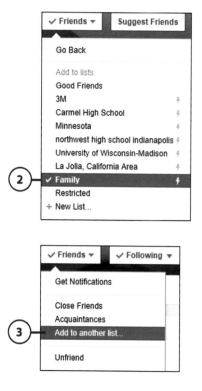

5 Click the privacy button, click More Options, and then select Custom to display the Custom Privacy pane.

6 Go to the Don't Share This With section and enter Family into the These People or Lists box.

7 Click the Save Changes button.

8 By default, all new posts you make are sent to all of your friends *except* the family members in your new friends list. To send a post to your family members only, click the privacy button within the post, click More Options, and then click Family. (Note, however, that this setting stays set on "Family" on your next posts, until you change it back.)

Privacy Settings
Learn about Facebook's privacy settings in Chapter 9, "Managing Your Privacy on Facebook."

Share Photos and Videos

Just as you can read each other's status updates, you can also share photos and videos with your children and grandchildren.

To this end, you should encourage your grandkids or their parents to post photos and videos of themselves to Facebook. This provides you a constantly updated photo album of your loved ones.

You should also try to post the occasional photo or video of yourself, for your family members to see. Don't limit yourself to posed pictures, either; your grandkids especially will get a big kick out of any crazy or silly picture or video you upload.

Pictures and Movies

Learn more about sharing photos and videos in Chapter 10, "Viewing and Sharing Photos and Videos."

Chat via Text and Video

If you're on one side of the country and your kids and grandkids are on the other, or even if you're only a few states away, you might only see your family in person one or two times a year. With Facebook text and video chat, you can visit with each other several times a week, if you like. It can truly bring together distant families.

Chatting is easier if everybody expects it. To this end, try to schedule time for a weekly video chat with each of your children and grandchildren. This is especially great for talking to your younger grandkids who are sure to appreciate the one-on-one time with their favorite grandpa or grandma.

For the teenagers in your family, Facebook's text chat might be more up their alley. Chatting on Facebook is just like texting on a mobile phone, and you know your kids and grandkids are okay with that. Next time you're on Facebook, check to see if your favorite grandchild is also online and, if so, open a text chat and say hi. If she wants to turn it into a video chat, you always have that option.

Facebook Chat

Learn more about text and video chatting in Chapter 11, "Chatting in Real Time—via Text or Video."

Play Games Together

Here's one you might not have thought of. If your grandkids are like mine, they love to play games—board games, card games, video games, you name it. Well, Facebook is chock full of social games that you can play with other Facebook users. That means all you have to do is pick a game, and then invite your grandkids (or even your grown children) to play it with you, online.

What games are good to play with the younger members of your family? Board games are good, as are card games, word games, and trivia games. Just go to the Games Center page and search for games by name or type.

Facebook Games

Learn more about finding and playing Facebook games in Chapter 15, "Playing Games."

Five Things *Not* to Do with Your Kids and Grandkids on Facebook

If your children and grandchildren are still on Facebook, you need to make sure you don't drive them away with inappropriate (for them) behavior. With that in mind, here are some important things *not* to do when posting and responding to your kids and grandkids.

1. Don't friend their friends. Your kids and grandkids like to keep their friends and family separate, so a family member getting friendly with one of their peers is a big social no-no. Resist the urge to send a friend request to one of your children's or grandchildren's Facebook friends. It's okay for you to

accept a friend request if one of her friends invites you, but it's not okay for you to initiate the contact. In general, you should keep your circle of friends to your friends and immediate family, not to your grandchildren's friends.

2. **Don't post unflattering photos of them.** Family photos that you think are funny might not seem so funny to your kids or grandkids—especially when their friends see them. The problem comes if you upload an embarrassing photo to Facebook and tag a relative in it. Thus tagged, all her Facebook friends will see the photo, with the resulting mortification. Think twice before you post those "cute" photos, especially as they get older. And if you must post the photos, don't tag them by name. If they're not tagged, their friends probably won't see the photos—which is best for all concerned.

3. **Don't use their photo as your profile picture.** I know you're really proud of your grandkids, but you shouldn't appropriate their photos as your own. Many grandparents use photos of their grandkids as their own profile pictures, or as the cover images on their Timeline pages. That's not fair to your grandkids—and, to be fair, it looks kind of weird. Post your own photo as your profile picture, and be done with it.

4. **Don't post too much personal information.** Facebook is a great forum for keeping friends and family up-to-date on what's happening in your life, but that doesn't mean you need to post every little detail about what's happening. Your kids and grandkids, especially, will be embarrassed or even grossed out if you post all the fiddly details about your latest medical exam or (God forbid) romantic interlude. There's just some stuff that kids don't want to know, and you need to know that.

5. **Don't try to be cool.** I know, you want to fit in with the young generation today, but let's face it—you're not that young, and you're not that cool. Don't embarrass yourself by trying to use today's hip lingo, or even common Facebook abbreviations, such as LOL (laughing out loud). No matter how hip you think you might be, you'll still come off as an old fogey trying to act younger than you really are. Bottom line: When you're posting on Facebook, act your age. You've earned the privilege.

>>>Go Further
OTHER PLACES TO FIND YOUR KIDS AND GRANDKIDS ONLINE

So if all the hip young kids are leaving Facebook (or using it a lot less on a regular basis), where are they going? There's no one destination for your grandkids and their friends; the younger generation is splintering their time between a number of social media startups. Here are some of the more popular social media for millennials today:

- **Instagram** (www.instagram.com), a social network that lets users shoot and share photos and short videos from their mobile phones.
- **Kik** (www.kik.com), a smartphone app that lets users send text and photo messages to their friends and family members.
- **Pinterest** (www.pinterest.com), a visual social network that lets users post pictures they find on the Web onto visual "pinboards," organized by topic.
- **Snapchat** (www.snapchat.com), an image-based smartphone messaging app that erases all posts after they've been viewed.
- **Tumblr** (www.tumblr.com), which lets users create short blog posts and share them across the network.
- **Twitter** (www.twitter.com), a kind of cross between an instant messaging service and a full-blown social network; users post short (140-character max) text messages, called *tweets*, that are then broadcast publicly to that person's followers on the service.
- **Vine** (www.vine.co), which lets users shoot looping, six-second video clips and share them publicly and with friends.
- **WhatsApp** (www.whatsapp.com), another smartphone app that lets users send and receive text, audio, video, and photo messages.

Of all these services, Twitter and Instagram are the most popular among teens and millennials. I'll be honest, however; you won't find a lot of people aged 50 and up on most of these newer social networks—which is why they're so appealing to younger users. Still, if you know your kids and grandkids are big on Twitter or Instagram and you want to stay in touch, you might want to investigate.

Security Settings

Login Alerts	Get an alert when anyone logs into your account from an unrecognized device or browser	Edit
Login Approvals	Use your phone as an extra layer of security to keep other people from logging into your account.	Edit
Code Generator	Use your Facebook app to get security codes when you need them.	Edit
App Passwords	Use special passwords to log into your apps instead of using your Facebook password or Login Approvals codes.	Edit
Public Key	Manage an OpenPGP key on your Facebook profile and enable encrypted notifications	Edit
Trusted Contacts	Pick friends you can call to help you get back into your account if you get locked out.	Edit
Your Browsers and Apps	Review which browsers you saved as ones you often use	Edit
Where You're Logged In	Review and manage where you're currently logged into Facebook.	Edit
Legacy Contact	Choose a family member or close friend to care for your account if something happens to you.	Edit
Deactivate Your Account	Choose whether you want to keep your account active or deactivate it.	Edit

Sidebar menu:

- General
- Security
- Privacy
- Timeline and Tagging
- Blocking
- Language
- Notifications
- Mobile
- Followers
- Apps
- Ads
- Payments
- Support Inbox
- Videos

Settings

- General
- Security
- Privacy
- Timeline and Tagging
- Location
- Blocking
- Language
- Notifications
- Text Messaging
- Followers
- Apps
- Ads

In this chapter, you learn how to configure various aspects of your Facebook account.

→ Changing Your Account Settings
→ Leaving Facebook
→ Dealing with Death

Managing Your Facebook Account—Even When You're Gone

Your Facebook account contains your basic personal information—your name, email address, password, and the like. What do you do if you move, get a new email account, or find that your password is compromised? Fortunately, Facebook lets you easily change any and all of this information, at any time.

Changing Your Account Settings

You can change all your Facebook settings from the Account Settings page on either the Facebook website or the mobile app.

Access Account Settings on the Facebook Website

If you're using Facebook on your notebook or desktop computer, you access the Account Settings page from the Facebook toolbar.

(1) Click the down arrow on the far right of the Facebook toolbar to display the menu of options.

(2) Click Settings to display the Account Settings page.

(3) Click the desired tab on the left to edit that type of information.

Create Page

Create Group
New Groups   4

Create Ads
Advertising on Facebook

Activity Log
News Feed Preferences
Settings

- General
- Security

- Privacy
- Timeline and Tagging
- Blocking
- Language

- Notifications
- Mobile
- Followers

- Apps
- Ads
- Payments
- Support Inbox
- Videos

Access Account Settings in the Facebook Mobile App

If you're using Facebook on your smartphone or tablet, you access the Account Settings page from the More menu. (Here's how it looks on an Android phone; the steps are similar on an iPhone or iPad.)

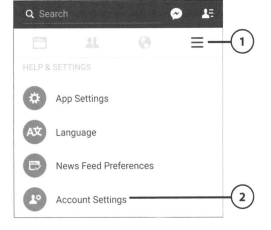

1. Tap More.

2. Scroll down to the Help & Settings section and tap Account Settings.

Configure Specific Settings

Once you display the Account Settings page, you click a specific tab (or, in the mobile app, tap a specific option) to view and edit that type of information.

All the available settings are detailed in the following table. Note that the settings differ somewhat between the website and the mobile app, so those settings with an asterisk (*) are available only on the Facebook website.

Facebook Account Settings

Type	Setting	Description
General	Name	Your real name.
	Username*	The nickname you use on the Facebook site.
	Contact (in the mobile app, separate Email and Phone settings)	Your email address and mobile phone number.
	Password	The password you use to log into Facebook.

Type	Setting	Description
	Networks	Manage your Facebook networks. (A Facebook network is like a group for people who attended a specific school or worked at a given company. To join a network, you must have an official email address from that school or company.)
	Temperature*	Fahrenheit or Celsius.
Security	Login Alerts	Receive an alert when anyone logs into your account from an unrecognized device or browser.
	Login Approvals	Require a phone-based approval when logging in. (This creates an extra layer of security.)
	Code Generator*	Use the Facebook app to generate security codes when necessary.
	App Passwords	Use different passwords instead of the Facebook password to log into apps.
	Public Key*	Manage levels of data encryption.
	Trusted Contacts	Specify friends you can call for help if you get locked out of your account.
	Your Browsers and Apps* (titled Recognized Devices in mobile app)	Review which browsers are saved as those you most often use.
	Where You're Logged In* (titled Your Active Sessions in mobile app)	Review where you've recently logged into Facebook.
	Legacy Contact	Choose a friend or family member to manage your account in case something happens to you. (Such as death—discussed later in this chapter.)
	Deactivate Your Account	Disable your Facebook account.
Privacy	Who can see my stuff?	Determine who can see your future posts, review all posts you're tagged in, and limit the audience for past posts.

Type	Setting	Description
	Who can contact me?	Determine who can send you friend requests.
	Who can look me up?	Determine who can look you up using the email address and phone number you've provided, as well as whether web search engines can link to your profile.
Timeline and Tagging	Who can add things to my timeline?	Determine who can post to your Timeline and lets you review posts you're tagged in before they appear.
	Who can see things on my timeline?	Review what others see on your Timeline, and determine who can see posts (and what others post) on your Timeline.
	How can I manage tags people add and tagging suggestions?	Review tags to your own posts, posts you're tagged in, and tag suggestions to photos.
Location (in mobile app only)	Nearby Friends	Let Facebook friends know when you're nearby
	Place Tips	Display tips about nearby places in your News Feed
	Location History	When active, lets Facebook build a history of locations you've visited.
	Location Services	Enables your mobile device's location services (or takes you to phone location settings).
	Wi-Fi (Android only)	Enables your mobile device's Wi-Fi functionality.
Blocking	Restricted List*	Edit your list of user restrictions.
	Block Users	Block specific users from seeing or contacting you.
	Block Messages*	Block specific users from sending you text or video messages.
	Block App Invites*	Block app requests from specific users.
	Block Event Invites*	Block event invitations from specific users.
	Block Apps*	Block apps from appearing in your News Feed.
	Block Pages*	Block interaction with specific Facebook Pages.

Type	Setting	Description
Language	What language do you want to use Facebook in?*	Show Facebook in a designated language.
	What language do you want stories to be translated into?	Specify a translated language for foreign-language posts.
	What languages do you understand?	Tell Facebook which languages you can read.
	What languages do you not want automatically translated?	Tell Facebook which languages to not translate into your main language.
Notifications	On Facebook	Manage notifications from within the Facebook website.
	Email	Manage account-related email messages.
	Desktop and Mobile	Manage notifications on either your mobile device or computer.
	Text Message	Receive notifications via text message.
	What Notifications You Get (in mobile app only)	Determine which notifications you see in mobile app.
Mobile	Mobile Settings*	Register your mobile phone to receive text messages from Facebook (or not).
Text Messaging (in mobile app only)	Current Phone Numbers	Manage your registered mobile phone numbers.
	Text Messaging	Register your phone to receive text messages from Facebook.
	Mobile PIN	Register a PIN instead of a password for the mobile app.
	Notifications	Determine which notifications you receive.
	Daily Text Limit	Determine how many text messages you can receive from Facebook per day.
Followers	Who Can Follow Me	Determine who (beside your Facebook friends) can follow your posts.
	Follower Comments	Determine who can comment on your posts.
	Follower Notifications*	Get notifications when people who aren't your friends follow you or share your posts.

Type	Setting	Description
	Comment Ranking*	When enabled, displays most relevant comments first.
	Username*	Specify a Facebook username.
	Twitter*	Connect a Twitter account to your Facebook account.
	Follow Plugin*	Add a Facebook Follow button to your website, if you have one.
Apps	Logged in with Facebook	Manage those apps that you use Facebook to log into.
	Apps, Websites, and Plugins (in the mobile app, titled Platforms)	Lets you use apps, plugins, games, and websites on Facebook.
	Apps Others Use	Control the level of information that your friends' apps can retrieve from your account.
	Old Versions of Facebook for Mobile	Control the privacy of posts made in older mobile versions of Facebook.
Ads	Ads based on my use of websites and apps	Determines what types of personalized ads Facebook displays.
	Ads on apps and websites off of the Facebook Companies	Determines whether your Facebook information can be used to show you ads on other websites.
	Ads with my social actions	Determines who can see ads (and your implicit recommendations) based on Facebook Pages you visit.
	Ads based on my preferences	Manage the preferences Facebook uses to show you ads.
Payments	Payment History (in the mobile app, Purchase History)	View your Facebook Payments purchase history. (Facebook Payments is a site-specific virtual currency used for in-app and in-game purchase.)
	Account Settings (in the mobile app, Preferred Currency)	Manage your payment methods, password, and preferred currency.
	Account Balance (mobile app only)	View your Facebook Payments account balance.

Type	Setting	Description
Support Inbox	Support Inbox	Contact Facebook technical support.
Videos*	Video Default Quality*	For the Facebook website, determine the resolution of video playback.
	Auto-Play Videos*	Determine whether videos in your desktop News Feed play automatically.

Leaving Facebook

If you ever choose to leave Facebook, you have two options. You can *deactivate* your account, which temporarily hides your account information from others, or you can *delete* your account, which permanently removes your account information.

Deactivate Your Account

Deactivating your account is meant as a temporary solution that you can undo at any future point. When you deactivate your account, Facebook doesn't actually delete your account information; it merely hides it so others can't view it. Because your account information still exists, it's simple enough to reactivate a deactivated account.

1. Click the down arrow on the far right of the Facebook toolbar and then click Settings. (In the mobile app, tap More and then tap Account Settings or Settings, Account Settings.)

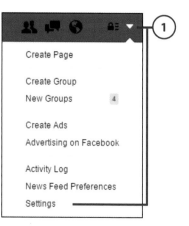

(2) Click the Security tab in the left column to display the Security Settings page.

(3) Scroll to the bottom of the page and click Deactivate Your Account.

(4) When this section expands, click the Deactivate Your Account link.

(5) When prompted, enter your Facebook password and click Continue.

(6) On the next page, Facebook gives you several reasons to stay. You can ignore these. Instead, scroll to the Reason for Leaving section and select why it is you're leaving. This is a requirement; you have to tell Facebook something here.

They'll Miss You!

Facebook really, really doesn't want to see you leave, so it tugs at your heartstrings by showing you pictures of some of your Facebook friends with the messages "Bob will miss you," "Dinah will miss you," and so forth. If you truly want to leave, resist the urge to change your mind.

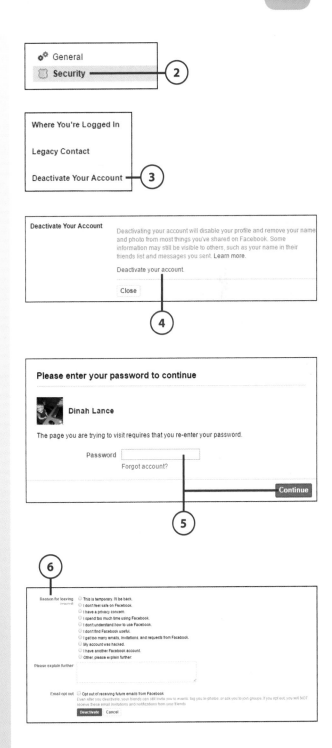

⑦ Check the Email Opt Out box if you don't want to be hounded by Facebook to venture back into the fold.

⑧ Click the Deactivate button to deactivate your account.

Facebook Messenger

If you're using the Messenger app on your mobile device, you'll see an option that lets you continue to use that app for text and video chats. If you want to stop using Messenger, too, uncheck the Keep Me Signed Into Messenger option.

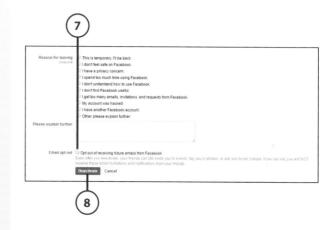

Permanently Delete Your Facebook Account

If you're absolutely, positively sure you'll never want to be a Facebook user again—and you want more reassurance that your personal data has been wiped—then you want to permanently delete your account. This is more difficult to do than deactivating your account for the simple reason that your Facebook account is likely connected to lots of other websites.

It's Not All Good

It's Final

Deleting your Facebook account is final; all your status updates and other information will be permanently erased. If you later want to rejoin Facebook, you'll have to start completely from scratch.

1. Go to each website you've linked to your Facebook account and disconnect the link—that is, create a new login ID that is not related to your Facebook ID. Do *not* log into these sites with your Facebook account!

2. Log in to your Facebook account and go to Facebook's Delete My Account page (www.facebook.com/help/delete_account). You have to enter this URL directly into your web browser; there's no link to this page from within Facebook.

3. Click the Delete My Account button to display the Permanently Delete Account dialog box.

4. Enter your Facebook password into the Password box, perform the security check, and then click OK.

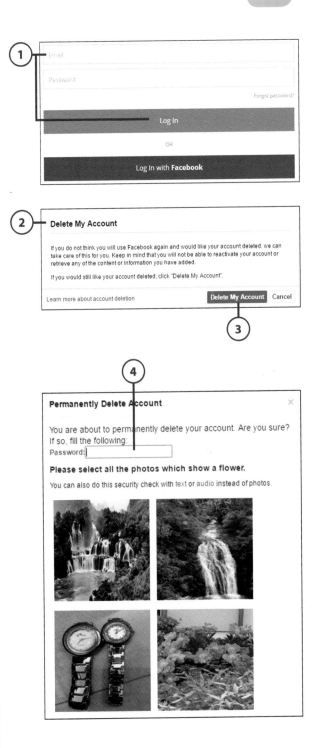

It's Not All Good

14 Days

When you follow this procedure, Facebook deletes your account—so long as you don't log back in to Facebook or log onto any websites that you log into with your Facebook account for the next 14 days. Any interaction with your Facebook account during this 14-day period reactivates your account. This also means not clicking the Facebook Like button on any other website.

Dealing with Death

Here's a question none of us want to face but all of us will have to: What happens to your Facebook account when you die?

The legal status of one's online accounts is a growing issue as online users age. After all, only you are supposed to have access to your online accounts; only you know your password to get into Facebook, Twitter, or even your online banking site (although you could share these with a loved one, for security purposes). And if you aren't able to get online, because you're dead, how can your accounts be put on hold or deleted?

Facebook, fortunately, has considered this situation and offers several options for accounts belonging to deceased members: You can memorialize the account, or you can simply remove it from the Facebook site.

Memorialize an Account

If you choose to memorialize the deceased's account, Facebook retains that person's Timeline page but locks it so that no one can log into it, and so no new friends can be accepted. Current friends, however, can share memories of the deceased on the memorialized timeline, and all existing content remains available for friends to view. (Who can view it depends on the Timeline's existing privacy settings.)

Anyone can report a deceased user to Facebook, and thus begin the memorialization process.

(1) From your web browser, go to www.facebook.com/help/contact/234739086860192 to display Facebook's Memorialization Request page.

(2) Enter the full name of your loved one into the Who Passed Away? box.

(3) Enter the date of this person's death into the When Did They Pass Away? box.

(4) If you have this information, enter a link to any online information reporting this person's death into the Proof of Death box. You can link to this person's online obituary or memorial page from the attending funeral home.

(5) Click the Send button.

It's Not All Good

Mistaken Memorialization

What do you do if someone memorializes your account—either on purpose or by mistake—and you're not dead yet? You need to contact Facebook via a special form to say you're still alive and want to continue using your account. You won't be able to log into Facebook if your account is in a memorialized state, so go to www.facebook.com/help/contact/292558237463098 and fill out the form there.

Name a Legacy Contact

You can prepare for the inevitable (and make things easier for your surviving friends and family) by designating someone to manage your Facebook account after your passing. This person will be your account's legacy contact, and can handle all the details involved with memorializing your account.

(1) Click the down arrow on the far right of the Facebook toolbar and then click Settings.

(2) Click the Security tab on the left.

(3) Click Legacy Contact to expand that section.

(4) Click within the Choose a Friend box and enter your friend's name. As you type, matching names are displayed; click the friend you want.

(5) Click the Add button; this displays a message to the person you selected.

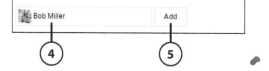

6 Edit the default message if you like and then click the Send button.

7 Check the box in the Data Archive Permission section to let your legacy contact download a copy of what you've shared on Facebook, including photos and videos.

8 Check the box in the Account Deletion section if you want your account removed after you pass away.

9 Check the box in the Legacy Contact Reminder section if you want to be reminded of your legacy contact once a year.

10 Click the Close button.

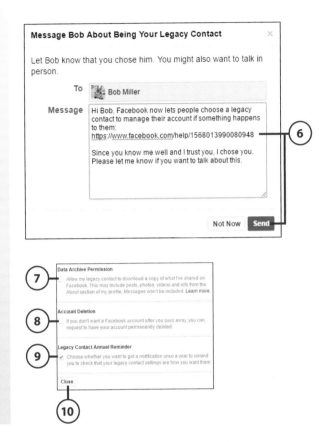

Remove an Account

If you'd rather not have a loved one's Facebook account memorialized, you can ask Facebook to remove the person's account from the site. Believe it or not, this is a more involved process than memorializing the account.

In preparation for this process, you need some proof of the person's death, typically a copy of the death certificate. This documentation needs to be scanned into your computer as an image file that you can upload to Facebook when required.

(1) From your web browser, go to www.facebook.com/help/contact/228813257197480 to display the Special Request for Deceased Person's Account page.

(2) Enter your name into the Your Full Name box.

(3) Enter the deceased's name into the If You're Friends With This Person on Facebook... box.

(4) Enter the name the deceased used on Facebook into the Full Name on the Deceased Person's Account box.

(5) Enter the URL of the deceased person's Timeline page into the Web Address (URL) of the Deceased Person's Timeline box.

(6) Enter the email address used by the deceased person (if you know it) into the Account Email Address of the Deceased Person box.

(7) Go to the How Can We Help You? section and select the Please Remove This Account option.

(8) In the When Did This Person Pass Away? section, provide the deceased user's year of death.

(1) (2)

Special Request for Deceased Person's Account

Please use this form to request the removal of a deceased person's account or for memorialization special requests. We extend our condolences and appreciate your patience and understanding throughout this process. Unrelated inquires received through this channel may not receive a response. To protect the privacy of people on Facebook, we cannot provide anyone with login information for accounts.

Your full name

Please note that we require verification that you are an immediate family member or executor for account removal or special requests.

If you're friends with this person on Facebook, please enter their name in the box below

Full name on the deceased person's account

(3) (4)

Web address (URL) of the deceased person's timeline
https://www.facebook.com/...

Account email address of the deceased person
The email that may have been used to create the account

How can we help you?
  Please memorialize this account
  Please remove this account
  I have a special request
  I have a question

When did the person pass away?
+ Add year

(9) You need to provide some proof of the person's death—ideally, a scan or photo of the death certificate. Click the Choose File button and then select the file for the death certificate or other document.

(10) When you return to the Special Request for Deceased Person's Account page, enter any additional comments or requests into the Additional Information box.

(11) Click the Send button.

(9)

To help quickly process your request, please provide a scan or photo of your loved one's death certificate.

If you don't have your loved one's death certificate, please visit the Help Center to learn about the other types of documentation we accept.

[Choose File] No file chosen

Additional information

If you have a special request or question, please use this space to provide more information

Send

(10)

(11)

Download Content from a Deceased Person's Account

Most Facebook users put a large chunk of their lives online, in the form of photos, videos, and such. Rather than abandon those photos and other content when a loved one dies, you can ask to download that content for your own use.

Due to privacy concerns, which continue after a person's death, this process is somewhat involved—unless you've named a legacy contact. If you have a legacy contact, Facebook will contact this person with instructions on how to download all your shared Facebook data.

If a user hasn't named a legacy contact, a family member or close friend can retrieve that person's data after death, but with some effort. This person will need a scan of their driver's license or other government-issued ID scanned to upload to Facebook when asked; she'll also need to scan a copy of the deceased person's death certificate.

1. From your web browser, go to www.facebook.com/help/contact/398036060275245 to display the Requesting Content From a Deceased Person's Account page.

2. Click Yes that you're an authorized representative of the deceased person. The page expands.

3. If the person is a minor, check Yes. Otherwise, check No. The page expands.

4. When you're asked if you have a will or power of attorney that specifically addressed this person's Facebook account, click Yes if you do and No if you don't.

5. If you clicked Yes, send a certified copy of that document and a court order referencing the disclosure of this and other electronic content to the following address:

Facebook Security
1601 Willow Road
Menlo Park, CA 94025

Requesting Content From a Deceased Person's Account

Please use this form to request content from a deceased person's account. We extend our condolences and appreciate your patience and understanding throughout this process.

Are you an authorized representative of the deceased person?
- Yes
- No

Is the deceased person a minor?
- Yes
- No

Do you have a legal document like a will, a durable power of attorney or other document executed by the deceased person establishing that the deceased person wished to specifically release their electronic communications to you or another person?
- Yes
- No

We will need a certified copy of that document and a court order referencing disclosure of electronic communications to continue evaluating your request. Please mail both to us at:

Facebook Security
1601 Willow Road
Menlo Park, CA 94025

6 If you clicked no, check to accept the disclaimer. (You'll also need to accept the disclaimer if you checked yes.)

7 Enter your name into the Your Full Name box.

8 Enter your street address into the Your Mailing Address box.

9 Enter your email address into the Your Email Address box.

10 In the Photocopy of Your Government-Issued Photo ID section, click Choose Files to upload a scan of your driver's license or other identification.

11 Enter the deceased's email address or a link to their Facebook Timeline page.

12 In the Any Documents Establishing Your Connection to the Deceased Person section, click the Choose Files button and select the file(s) required.

13 In the Copy of the Deceased Person's Death Certificate section, click the Choose Files button and select the file for the scanned-in death certificate.

14 Click the Send button. Facebook now evaluates your request and will eventually respond with further instructions.

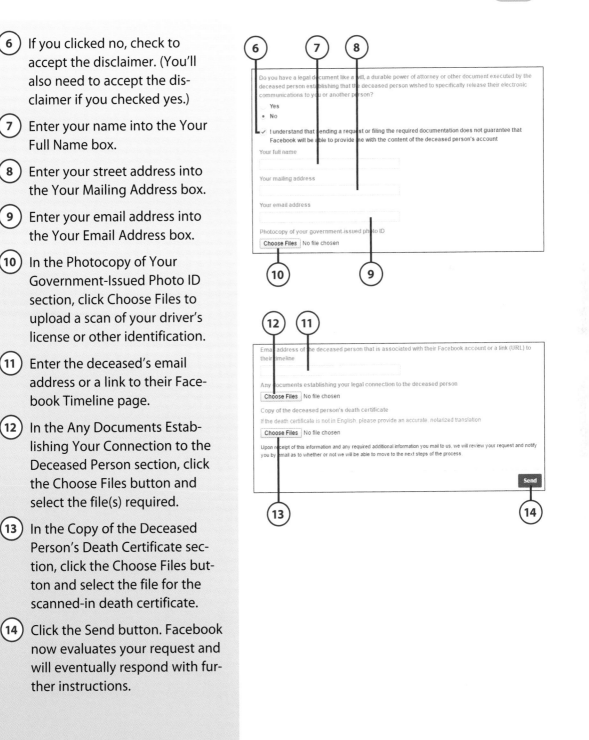

It's Not All Good

Incapacitated Users

The situation is less clear if you're still alive but incapacitated, without the ability to sign onto Facebook on your own behalf. At present, Facebook offers no formal process for a spouse or other family member to access an incapacitated user's account. The best thing to do, if you can, is have the person give you his password, and then log onto his account yourself, on his behalf. You can then delete or deactivate the account, as per the incapacitated user's request.

If your loved one is unable to provide you with his Facebook password, the situation is much more murky. You can try contacting Facebook on the behalf of your loved one, but it's unclear whether Facebook has the right to let you access that person's account. But it's worth trying.

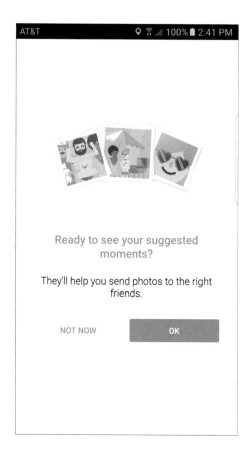

Ready to see your suggested moments?

They'll help you send photos to the right friends.

NOT NOW   OK

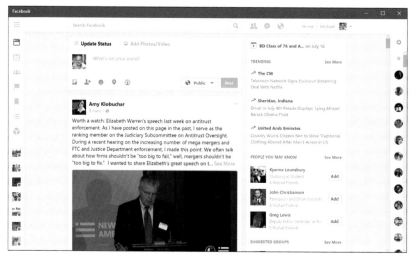

In this chapter, you learn about Facebook's
Moments mobile app and its Windows 10 app.

→ Using the Moments App
→ Using Facebook's Windows 10 App

Discovering Facebook's Other Apps

The Facebook and Messenger apps aren't the only apps that Facebook offers to mobile users. Facebook also offers the Moments app, which lets you manage and share the photos you take on your smartphone. Plus, if you have Windows 10 installed on your notebook or desktop computer, Facebook offers a Windows 10–specific app for accessing its service. We'll look at all these apps in this chapter.

Using the Moments App

First up is Facebook's Moments app. When you post photos to Facebook, you might have seen notices for this app that purports to make it easier to share your pictures with your Facebook friends. The Moments app lets you share photos stored on your phone with your Facebook friends, as well as see those photos stored on your friends' phones. Moments also synchronizes all your phone's photos with your Facebook photo albums.

You can even use Moments to group photos based on who is in them (using facial recognition technology) and where they were taken. Sharing a photo with someone in one of your photos is as easy as tapping the friend's name—and your friend can add her own photos of a given event to your own moment.

You can find Moments in your phone's app store. Facebook offers versions of the Moments app for both iOS and Android devices. I show you how to use the Android version here, although the iOS version (for Apple's iPhones) works similarly.

Collecting Moments

In Facebook parlance, a "moment" is a collection of photos based on something in common—maybe they were taken at the same place or event, or include the same people.

View and Share Suggested Moments

Facebook automatically gathers similar photos into suggested moments, which you can then edit and share with others.

1. Tap the Home icon to display the home screen in Moments.

2. You see a stack of selected moments. Swipe left on the top moment to view other moments underneath.

3. Tap See All to view all suggested moments in a scrolling list.

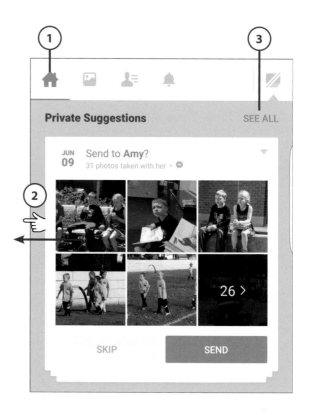

4 Tap a moment to open it for editing.

5 All photos in the moment are selected by default. Tap to deselect any photo you don't want to include.

6 Tap the To field to view a list of your Facebook friends.

Suggested Recipients

Based on who is in a group of photos, Facebook may suggest a recipient to share with. You can accept this person, or tap the To field to select other Facebook friends.

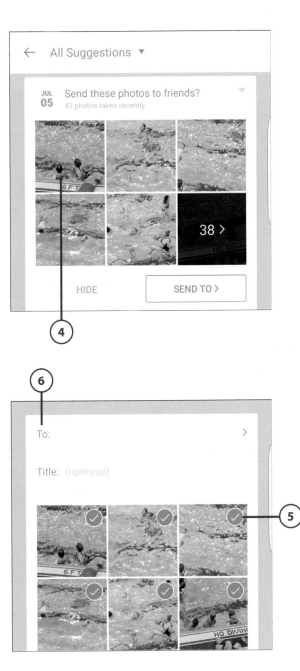

7 Tap to select who you want to share this moment with.

8 Tap Done.

9 Tap the Title field to add an optional title for this moment.

10 Tap Send to send this moment to the selected friend(s).

New to Moments

If a friend you share a moment with doesn't yet have the Moments app installed, she receives a message with a link to download the app.

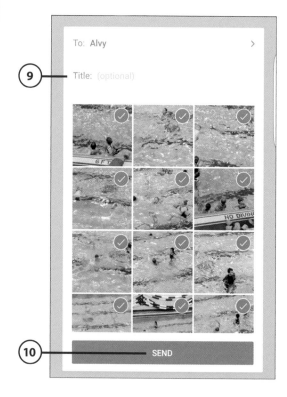

Create a New Moment

There are several ways to create a new moment. The easiest is to pick a specific friend, place, or photo and let Facebook assemble related photos.

(**1**) Tap the Home icon to display the home screen.

(**2**) Tap the blue + to create a new moment.

(**3**) You now see all the photos on your phone, grouped by date and location. Tap to select those photos you want to include in this new moment.

(**4**) Tap Next.

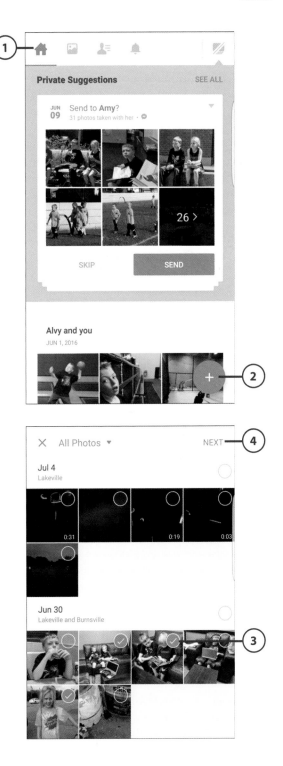

(5) Tap Moment Title and enter a title for this moment.

(6) Tap Next.

(7) Tap to select who you want to share this moment with.

(8) Tap Send to share this moment.

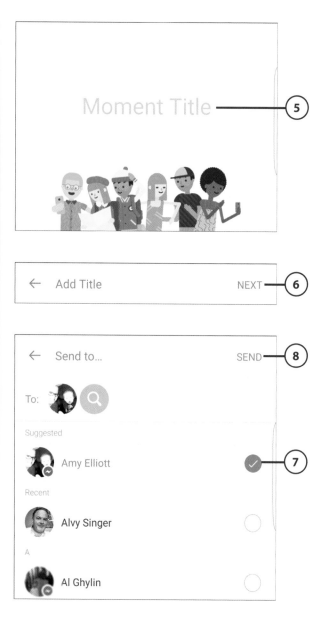

Request Photos from a Friend

You can also use the Moments app to request photos that any of your Facebook friends have taken.

(1) Tap the Friends icon to display a list of your Facebook friends.

(2) Tap the Ask button beside the friend's name.

(3) When prompted, enter a note explaining which photos you'd like to see.

(4) Tap Send.

Facebook Messenger
If your friend does not yet have the Moments app installed, she'll receive a message via Facebook Messenger to install Moments.

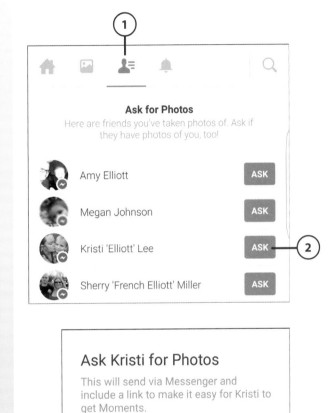

Using Facebook's Windows 10 App

If your personal computer is running the Windows 10 operating system, you're probably familiar with what Microsoft variable calls Universal Windows Platform (UWP) or just plain universal apps. A UWP app is designed to run across all Windows 10 devices and provide a more cohesive operating experience than traditional desktop apps or websites.

Not surprisingly, Facebook offers a UWP app for Windows 10. Also not surprisingly, it mirrors the Facebook website in terms of features and functionality.

Windows Store

You can download the Facebook app (for free!) from the Windows Store. Just click the Store icon on the Windows 10 taskbar and search for Facebook.

Navigate Facebook's Windows 10 App

Facebook's Windows 10 app looks a lot like the Facebook website, but it's somewhat streamlined. Navigating the app is also similar to navigating the website.

Notifications

When you install Facebook's Windows 10 app, all your Facebook notifications appear in the Windows 10 Notifications panel, as well as within the app itself.

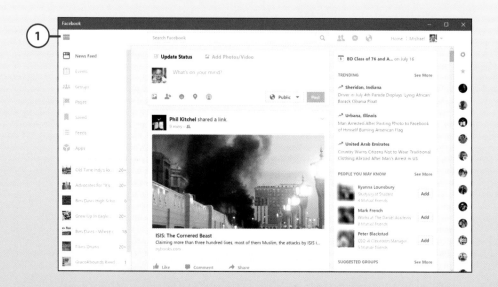

1 Click the Menu (hamburger) icon in the top-left corner to expand or contract the navigation sidebar. (The contracted sidebar takes up less space by displaying only icons; the expanded sidebar is easier to navigate because it includes labels for each item.)

(2) Click News Feed in the sidebar (or Home in the toolbar) to return to your home page and News Feed.

(3) Click within the Publisher box to post a new status update.

(4) Scroll down to read more posts in your News Feed.

(5) Click Friends Requests in the toolbar to view friend requests and suggested friends.

(6) Click Messages in the toolbar to view private messages and chats.

(7) Click Notifications to view notifications from Facebook.

(8) Click your name to view your Timeline page.

(9) Click the down-arrow next to your picture to configure settings and view other system preferences.

(10) Click a friend's picture in the Chat bar on the right to initiate a private chat with that person.

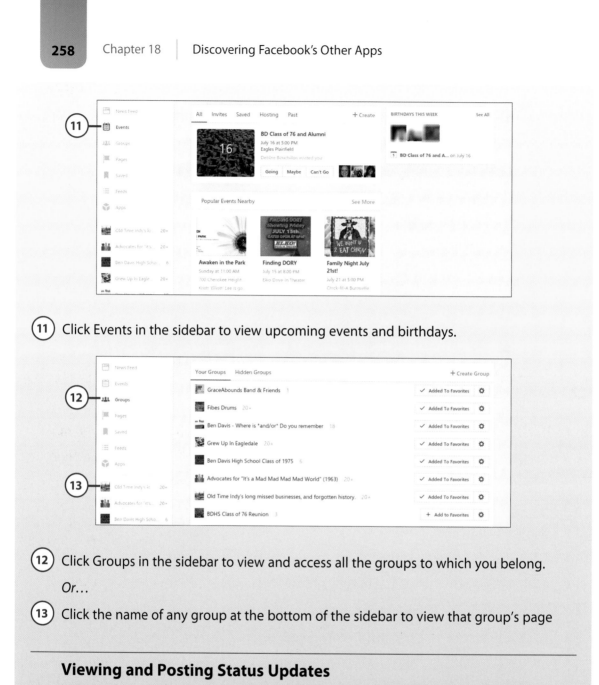

(11) Click Events in the sidebar to view upcoming events and birthdays.

(12) Click Groups in the sidebar to view and access all the groups to which you belong.

Or...

(13) Click the name of any group at the bottom of the sidebar to view that group's page

Viewing and Posting Status Updates

Reading, liking, sharing, and commenting on posts in your News Feed are identical to doing so on the Facebook website. It's the same with creating new status updates: just type your text into the Publisher box and add any photos, tags, check ins, and the like.

Glossary

Activity Log　A chronological list of all your activity on the Facebook site, including status updates, comments on others' posts, and more.

album　A collection of photos or videos uploaded to Facebook.

blog　A website where the owner writes about his own personal experiences and opinions, typically in short, frequent posts.

chat　Private messaging between two or more users.

Chat bar　Click to display a list of Facebook friends who are currently online and available for chatting.

Check In　A feature of Facebook that lets you identify your current location.

clickbait　A post or article that attempts to "bait" you into clicking to learn more.

Comment　Your personal reply to a Facebook post.

countdown list　A quasi-informational post or article that purports to tell you X number of things about a given topic.

cover image   The large "banner" photograph that displays across the top of your Timeline page.

emoji   A small image or icon that conveys an emotion or idea.

event   A Facebook page devoted to a particular online or real-world occasion. You can invite your Facebook friends to events you create.

Facebook Messenger   Facebook's mobile app for public and private messaging.

Facebook Moments   A mobile app that lets you share photos with your Facebook friends.

Facebook Slideshow   A mobile app that that enables you to create and share slideshows from your Facebook photos.

Facebook toolbar   The collection of clickable icons that appears at the top of every Facebook page.

Facebook   The world's largest social network, with more than one billion users.

friend request   An invitation to join a user's friends list.

friend   On Facebook, a user with whom you share posts. Users have to agree to join your friends list, by accepting a friend request.

Game Center   The hub for all social games on Facebook.

Group   A Facebook page devoted to a specific topic or community of users.

hashtag   A word or phrase that starts with the hash (#) character and describes the content of your post—and that readers can click to see similar posts with the same hashtag.

Instagram   A social network that lets users share photos and short videos from their mobile phones.

Kik   A smartphone app that lets users send text and photo messages to their friends and family members.

legacy contact   A friend or family member designated to manage your Facebook account after your death.

lightbox   A photo-viewing window superimposed over the normal News Feed.

Like   Giving a virtual "thumbs up" if you approve of a Facebook post—or, in the case of company or celebrity Pages, a way to follow posts from that entity.

link   A clickable link to a web page outside the Facebook site.

LinkedIn   A social network for business professionals.

meme   A concept or catchphrase or image that spreads in a viral fashion over the Internet.

Messages   Facebook's private messaging system.

mobile app   A software application for smartphone or tablet. Facebook offers several mobile apps for users.

mobile website   The version of the Facebook website that displays when you access facebook.com from a mobile device.

Most Recent   A view of the Facebook News Feed that displays the most recent posts from your friends.

navigation sidebar   The list of links to various pages and services found on the left side of the Facebook website.

News Feed   A stream of status updates from a user's friends.

notification   A message or alert from Facebook.

On This Day   A new Facebook post that includes one or more posts from this same day in the past.

Page   A Facebook page for a celebrity, company, or other public figure or entity.

Pinterest   A visual social network that lets users post pictures they find on the web onto visual "pinboards," organized by topic.

post   See *status update.*

Privacy button   Click to determine who can see a given post or piece of information.

profile picture   The picture (typically of you) that displays on your Timeline page and accompanies all posts you make on the Facebook site.

Public   The privacy setting that enables anyone on Facebook to see a given post or piece of information.

Publisher box   Where you enter the text for a new status update.

share   On the Facebook site, reposting someone else's status update to your friends list.

Snapchat   An image-based smartphone messaging app that erases all posts after they've been viewed.

social game   A game you play online either against other Facebook users or by sharing information with other Facebook users.

social media   See *social network*

social network   An Internet-based service that hosts a community of users and makes it easy for those users to communicate with one another.

status update   A short message (with text and/or images and video) that updates friends on what a user is doing or thinking.

tag   Identifying a friend in post or photo.

Timeline   A user's personal page on the Facebook site.

Top Stories   A view of the Facebook News Feed that displays the most important posts from your friends.

Trending   A section on the Facebook home page that displays the most currently active or interesting topics.

Tumblr   A social network that lets users create short blog posts and share them across the network.

Twitter   A cross between an instant messaging service and a full-blown social network; users post short (140-character max) text messages, called *tweets*, that are then broadcast publicly to that person's followers on the service.

unfriend   The process of removing a person from your Facebook friends list.

URL   Uniform Resource Locator, the address of a web page.

video chat   A face-to-face onscreen chat between two users.

Vine   A mobile social network that lets users shoot looping, six-second video clips and share them publicly and with friends.

viral   A post, picture, or video that spreads quickly from person to person until thousands of people have seen it.

WhatsApp   A smartphone app that lets users send and receive text, audio, video, and photo messages.

Year in Review   A post that Facebook creates, near the end of the calendar year, that attempts to encapsulate your activities on the Facebook site throughout the year.

YouTube   The Internet's largest video sharing community.

Index

Symbols

(hashtags) in status updates, 97

A

abbreviations (shorthand), writing posts/status updates, 118-120
accepting
    event invitations, 197
    friend requests, 41-42
accessing
    accounts, 229
    Timelines, 46-47
accounts
    creating, 4-7
    deactivating, 234-235
    death and account status, 238-245
    deleting, 236-238, 241-243
    downloading content from deceased users account, 243-245
    incapacitated users and account status, 246
    linking, 155
    logging
        into, 8-9
        out of, 9
    managing, 227-228
    mobile apps
        accessing, 229
        configuring, 229-234
    security, 6
    settings, configuring, 227-228
acronyms, writing posts/status updates, 118-120
Activity Log, editing, 58

Add a Location to Post button, 188

Add Friends button, 40

albums
    photos
        adding location information to, 148-149
        deleting, 153
        high quality photos, 149
        uploading, 147-152
        viewing, 140
    videos, viewing, 141

alumni groups. *See* groups

Android
    Facebook on, 26-29
    Messenger app, 163-168

approving tags on photos, 132

apps
    cover images, adding, 52
    family games, 223
    friends
        accepting/declining requests, 41
        finding, 32-34
    Game Center, 208-209
        managing games, 211-213
        playing games, 210-211
    Kik Messenger, families and, 225
    Moments, 249-250, 253-255
    pictures, changing, 47-49
    status updates
        posting, 96-97
        viewing, 62-68
    Timelines, accessing, 46-47
    Twitter, families and, 225
    Windows 10, 255-258

attention-seeking posts/status updates, 116

auto playback, 138

B

birthdays, 195, 204
    privacy, 205
    viewing today's birthdays, 204-205

Browse Groups page, 183, 186

browsing
    Game Center, 208-209
        managing games, 211-213
        playing games, 210-211
    groups, 183-184

BuzzFeed, 88

C

cameras (web) and video chats, 171

canceling, events, 203

celebrity Facebook Pages
    liking, 175
    re-liking, 179
    searching, 173-177
    unliking, 179
    viewing, 175-176

cell phones
    Android, 26-29
    iPhone, 18-21
    Messenger app, 163-168
    photos, posting from, 146

chat
    groups, creating, 166-168
    installing, 170
    live text chats, 162
    Messenger app, 163-168
    text chats, 222
    video chats, 168-171, 222

Chat bar, 14

Check In feature (iPhone), 19

Choose a File to Upload (camera) button, 188

Choose File to Upload or Open dialog box, 50

Choose from My Photos panel, 53

classmates, searching, 38

clickbait, 87

Closed groups, 185

closing accounts, 234-235

clubs (groups), 181
   browsing, 183-184
   chats, creating, 166-168
   Closed groups, 185
   finding, 182-183
   friends, reconnecting friends via groups, 192
   group pages, 186-188
   joining, 185
   leaving, 191
   managing, 191
   members, 189
   notifications, 190
   Open groups, 185
   photos, 190
   Public groups, 185
   visiting, 186-187

College or University section (People You May Know section), 38

commenting
   on updates, 67
   on status updates, 74
   on videos, 141

company Facebook Pages
   creating, 176
   liking, 175
   re-liking, 179
   searching, 173-177
   unliking, 179
   viewing, 175-176

complaining in posts/status updates, 115

confessions in posts/status updates, 115

configuring
   accounts
      mobile apps, 229-234
      settings, 227
   auto playback, 138
   default privacy settings, 124-126
   News Feeds, preferences, 76-77

confirmation emails
   friend requests, 42
   for new Facebook accounts, 7

contacts, finding friends via email, 39

Contacts, 35

countdown lists, 87-88

counting
   friend requests, 12
   messages, 12

cover images
   adding to Timeline, 52-54
   Facebook requirements, 53
   repositioning-54

Create Album button, 148

creating Facebook accounts, 4-7

Current City section (People You May Know section), 37

customizing
New Feeds, 76-77
Timelines, 45-47, 50-53
cover images, 52-54
editing Activity Log, 58
privacy, 55-56
profile pictures, 47, 51
updating profile information, 54-55

D

deactivating accounts, 234-235.
See also deleting accounts
death and account status, 238-241
downloading content from accounts,
243-245
removing accounts, 241-243
declining
event invitations, 197
friend requests, 41-42
default privacy settings, 124-126
Delete Photo panel, 153
deleting, 236-238. See also deactivating
accounts
accounts, 241-243
friends, 42-43
games, 211-213
photos, 152-153
status updates, 57
URLs from posts, 98
demographics of Facebook, 215-217
dialog boxes
Choose File to Upload or Open, 50
Save As, 144

displays, widescreen, 14
downloading
apps. See apps
content from deceased users account,
243-245
photos, 143, 146

E

editing
Activity Log, 58
events, 203
profiles, 54-55
Timelines, 54-58
email
confirmation for new Facebook
accounts, 7
contacts, finding friends via, 39
signing into Facebook with, 6-8
embarrassing photos in posts/status
updates, 115
emojis, 66, 165
Employer section (People You May
Know section), 38
etiquette
family, posts/status updates from,
223-224
grandchildren, posts/status updates
from, 223-224
links, 117
photos, 117
posts
abbreviations (shorthand), 118-120
grammar, 118
misspellings, 118
writing posts, 117

status updates, 106
  abbreviations (shorthand), 118-120
  grammar, 118
  misspellings, 118
  writing updates, 117
events
  birthdays, 195, 204-205
  canceling, 203
  creating, 200-202
  defining, 199
  Events page, 197-199
  invitations, managing, 196-197
  joining, 197
  scheduling, 200, 203
    creating, 200-202
    sending invitations, 202
  scheduling from sidebar menu, 13
  types of, 199
  viewing from sidebar menu, 13

F

Facebook
  demographics of, 215-217
  friend suggestions, accepting, 37
  Messenger app, 163. *See* Messenger app
  YouTube, linking, 155
Facebook Pages, 173
  creating, 176
  liking, 175
  managing, 178
  re-liking, 179
  unliking, 179
  viewing, 175
  viewing favorite pages, 178
  viewing posts, 176

Facebook-generated content, 90-92
families
  family games, 223
  grandchildren, 217-224
  Kik Messenger, 225
  members as friends, 32
  Twitter, 225
Find Friends button, 11
finding
  friends, 32, 35-42
  games, 208-209
  groups, 182-183
flame wars, 115
following
  celebrities. *See* celebrities
  companies/public figures, 173-177
  Facebook Pages, 175
formatting Moments apps, 253
frequency of posts, 121
friends
  adding, 189
  contact, limiting, 128
  defining, 31-32
  family members as, 32
  finding, 32, 35-40
  friend requests, 34, 42
    accepting/declining, 41-42
    counting, 12
    Friend Requests button (toolbar), 11, 42
    managing, 128
  Friends button (toolbar), 36, 39
  Friends Lists, 219-220
  of friends, searching, 39-40
  grandchildren, 217-225
  groups, 192

photos, 142-143
  albums, 140
  downloading, 143
  sharing-144-152
  tagging, 150
  viewing, 136
refriending, 43
tagging in status updates, 95, 102
unfriending, 42-43
videos
  albums, 141
  chats, 168-171
  sharing, 144-152
  viewing, 137-139

G

Game Center
  browsing, 208-209
  games. *See also* games
    managing, 211-213
    playing, 210-211
games, 89-90
  family games, 223
  grandchildren, playing with, 223
  managing, 211-213
  playing, 207, 210-211
  privacy, 213
  searching, 208-209
  social games, 208
  types of, 208
gear (Settings) button, 9
general account settings, configuring, 228
grammar in posts/status updates, 118

grandchildren
  etiquette, 223-224
  friending, 217-218
  Friends Lists, creating, 219-220
  games, playing, 223
  Kik Messenger, 225
  posts, 219-220
  privacy, 220-221
  sharing photos/videos, 222
  status updates, 219-220
  text chats, 222
  Twitter, 225
  video chats, 222
groups, 181
  browsing, 183-184
  chats, creating, 166-168
  Closed groups, 185
  finding, 182-183
  friends, reconnecting friends via
    groups, 192
  group pages, 186-188
  joining, 185
  leaving, 191
  managing, 191
  members, 189
  notifications, 190
  Open groups, 185
  photos, 190
  Public groups, 185
  visiting, 186-187

H

hard-to-find friends, finding, 40
hashtags (#) in status updates, 97

hiding
   game posts, 90
   status updates, 57
high quality photos, 149
High School section (People You May
   Know section), 37
Home button, 11
home pages
   navigating, 10-11
   sidebar menus, 10-14
Hometown section (People You May
   Know section), 37

I

images
   adding information to, 148
   albums
      deleting, 153
      uploading, 147-152
      viewing, 140
   countdown lists, adding, 87-88
   cover images, 52-54
   deleting, 152-153
   downloading, 143
   embarrassing photos in posts/status
      updates, 115
   etiquette, 117
   friends
      photos, 142-143
      tagging, 150
   groups, 190
   high quality photos, 149
   lightboxes, 72
   location information, adding to, 149
   memes, adding, 83-85
   mobile apps, posting, 146
   Moments app, 249-250, 253-255
   News Feed, posting, 79, 83
   photo albums, 148-149
   posting to status updates, 79, 83, 99-100
   privacy, managing, 129-130
   profile pictures, 47
   sharing, 144-152, 222
   status updates, posting to, 145
   surveys, adding, 86-87
   tagging, approving, 132
   viewing, 64, 71, 136
incapacitated users and account status, 246
individual posts, privacy, 126-127
installing chat applets, 170
invitations. See also requests
   event invitations, 197
   friend requests, 34
   managing, 196
      replying, 196-197
      viewing events, 197-199
   sending, 202
iPad
   Facebook on, 22-24
   Messenger app, 163-168
iPhone
   Facebook on, 18-21
   Messenger app, 163-168

J

jobs, finding friends from, 38
joining
   events, 197
   groups, 185

K

Keep Me Logged In option, 9
Kik Messenger, families and, 225

L

law enforcement and posts/status
  updates, 115
leaving
    deactivating accounts, 234-235
    deleting accounts, 236-238
    groups, 191
left side menu, 10-12
legacy contacts, 240-241
legal status of accounts, death, 238-241
lightboxes, 72, 136
Like button, 175
liking
    Facebook Pages, 175
    status updates, 73
limiting contact with members, 128
LinkedIn, 4
linking
    accounts, 155
    Facebook with YouTube, 155
links
    etiquette, 117
    posting to status updates, 98
    viewing, 64, 71
    websites, 88
lists, creating friends, 219
live text chat, 162
live video, streaming, 156

locations
    adding to posts, 100-101
    photos, adding, 149
lock icon, 11
logging
    into/out of accounts, 8-9
    into iPhone, Facebook on, 18

M

managing
    accounts, 227-228
    Facebook Pages, 178
    games, 211-213
    groups, leaving, 191
    invitations, 196
        replying to, 196-197
        viewing events, 197-199
    pages, following, 178-179
    privacy
        limiting contact, 128
        posting, 131-132
        selecting who sees posts, 124-127
        tagging, 129-130
        Timelines, 133
manners
    family, posts/status updates from,
      223-224
    grandchildren, posts/status updates
      from, 223-224
    links, 117
    photos, 117
    posts
        abbreviations (shorthand), 118-120
        grammar, 118
        misspellings, 118
        writing posts, 117

status updates, 106
    abbreviations (shorthand), 118-120
    grammar, 118
    misspellings, 118
    writing updates, 117

Maybe status (event invitations), 197

meaningless posts/status updates, 116

members (groups)
    adding as friends, 189
    viewing, 189

memes, adding, 83-85

memorializing accounts, 238-241

menus, sidebar, 10-14, 69

messages
    birthdays, 205
    counting, 12
    email. *See* email
    group pages, 186-187
    Messages button (toolbar), 11
    privacy, 220-221
    private messages, 159
    sharing, 219-220
    text
        reading, 161
        sending, 159-165
        viewing, 162
    viewing from sidebar menu, 12

Messages button, 11

Messenger app, 163
    creating group chats, 166-168
    sending and receiving messages,
      163-165
    video chats, 169-170

microphones and video chats, 171

misspellings in posts/status updates, 118

mobile apps. *See also* apps
    accounts
        accessing, 229
        configuring, 229-234
    cover images, adding, 52
    friends
        accepting/declining requests, 41
        finding, 32-34
    pictures
        changing, 47-49
    status updates
        posting, 96
        viewing, 62-68
    Timelines, accessing, 46

mobile devices
    Android, 26-29
    iPad, 22-24
    iPhone, 18-21
    Messenger app, 163-168

Moments app, 249-250, 253-255

Most Recent Posts, viewing, 69-70

multiplayer games, 207

mutual friends, 37. *See also* friends

N

navigating
    apps
        Moments, 249-250, 253-255
        Windows 10, 255-258
    Facebook, 10-14
    home page, 10-11
    videos, 139

networks (social), goal of, 4

New Message button, 160

News Feeds, 4, 10
  Android, 26-29
  displaying, 68-69
  iPad, 22-24
  iPhone, 18-21
  memes, adding, 83-85
  personalizing, 75-77
  photos. *See also* photos
    albums, 140
    viewing, 136
  posts
    countdown lists, 87-88
    Facebook-generated content, 90-92
    games, 89-90
    linking websites, 88
    photos, 79, 83
    surveys, 86-87
    trending topics, 92
  reading from sidebar menu, 12
  videos, viewing, 137-139
  viewing, 62
nostalgia groups. *See* groups
notifications, 190
Notifications button, 11
Notifications button (toolbar), 11

O

occasions
  birthdays, 195, 204-205
  canceling, 203
  creating, 200-202
  defining, 199
  Events page, 197-199
  invitations, managing, 196-197
  joining, 197
    scheduling, 200, 203
      creating, 200-202
      sending invitations, 202
    scheduling from sidebar menu, 13
    types of, 199
    viewing from sidebar menu, 13
Only Me option (privacy), 56
Open groups, 185
opinions in posts/status updates, 115
organizations (groups), 181
  browsing, 183-184
  chats, creating, 166-168
  Closed groups, 185
  finding, 182-183
  friends, reconnecting friends via
    groups, 192
  group pages, 186-187
  joining, 185
  leaving, 191
  managing, 191
  members, 189
  notifications, 190
  Open groups, 185
  photos, 190
  Public groups, 185
  visiting, 186-187

P

Pages (Facebook), 173
  creating, 176
  liking, 175
  managing, 178
  re-liking, 179
  unliking, 179
  viewing, 175-178

passwords
creating, 6
security, 6

People screen (Messenger app), 165

People You May Know section, finding friends via
College or University section, 38
Current City section, 37
Employer section, 38
High School section, 37
Hometown section, 37
Mutual Friends section, 37

permanently deleting accounts, 236-238

personal information in posts/status updates, 115-116

personalizing
News Feeds, 75-77
Timeline, 45
cover images, 52-54
editing Activity Log, 58
privacy, 55-56
profile pictures, 47
updating profile information, 54-55

phones
contacts, finding friends, 35
photos, posting from, 146
Messenger app, placing calls from, 166

photos
adding information to, 148
albums
deleting, 153
uploading, 147-152
viewing, 140
countdown lists, adding, 87-88
cover images, 52-54
deleting, 152-153

downloading, 143
embarrassing photos in posts/status updates, 115
etiquette, 117
friends
photos, 142-143
tagging, 150
groups, 190
high quality photos, 149
lightboxes, 72
location information, adding to, 149
memes, adding, 83-85
mobile apps, posting, 146
Moments app, 249-250, 253-255
News Feed, posting, 79, 83
photo albums, 148-149
posting to status updates, 79, 83, 99-100
privacy, managing, 129-130
profile pictures, 47
sharing, 144-152, 222
status updates, posting to, 145
surveys, adding, 86-87
tagging, approving, 132
video slideshow of photos, 154
viewing, 64, 71, 136

pictures. *See* photos

Pinterest, 4

playing games, 210-211

police, posts/status updates, 115

Post button, 97, 188

posts
abbreviations (shorthand) in, 118-120
attention-seeking posts, 116
bad posts, avoiding, 114
personal information, 116
uninteresting/unwise posts, 115-116

birthdays, 205

complaining in, 115

confessions in, 115

etiquette, 106. *See also* manners

  abbreviations (shorthand), 118-120

  grammar, 118

  misspellings, 118

  writing posts, 117

Facebook Page posts, viewing, 176

family posts, etiquette and, 223-224

frequency of, determining, 121

friends, tagging, 102

good posts, writing, 111

  important information, 113-114

  interesting information, 112-113

grandchildren, 223-224

group pages, 186-187

law enforcement, 115

locations, 100-101

managing, 131-132

meaningless posts, 116

News Feeds

  adding, 83-85

  countdown lists, 87-88

  Facebook-generated content, 90-92

  games, 89-90

  linking websites, 88

  photos, 79, 83

  surveys, 86-87

  trending topics, 92

opinions in, 115

personal information in, 115-116

photos, embarrassing photos in posts, 115

privacy, 104-106, 125, 220-221

  confessions, 115

  personal information, 115-116

  selecting who sees, 124-127

promoted posts, 177

sharing, 93, 219-220

status updates, 98

  photos, 145

  pictures, 99-100

  videos, 145

telling friends what you're doing, 103

updates, 258

vague, 116

preferences, configuring News Feeds, 76-77

privacy

  birthdays, 205

  Check In feature (iPhone), 19

  contact, limiting, 128

  friend requests, managing, 128

  games, 213

  grandchildren, 220-221

  Only Me option, 56

  posting, managing, 131-132

  posts, 125

    confessions, 115

    personal information, 115-116

    selecting who sees, 124-127

  private messages, 159

  profile information, 55-56

  status updates, 104-106

    confessions, 115

    personal information, 115-116

  tagging, managing, 129-130

  Timelines, managing, 133

Privacy button, 59, 104

processing videos, 145

profiles

  editing information, 54-55

  privacy, 55-56

  profile pictures, changing, 47

  updating information, 54-55

promoted posts, 177

public figures, searching, 173-177

Public groups, 185

Publisher box, 97

R

reading text messages, 161

receiving text messages, 163-165

refriending friends, 43

re-liking Facebook Pages, 179

removing. *See also* deleting
    accounts upon users death, 241-243
    friends, 42-43
    photos, 143
    your name from friends photos, 143

replying to
    event invitations, 196-197
    group posts, 187

repositioning cover images, 54

requests (friend)
    accepting, 41-42
    counting, 12
    Friend Requests toolbar, 11
    invitations, 34
    Moments app, 255

responding to
    event invitations, 196-197
    group posts, 187

right side menu, 14

S

Save As dialog box, 144

Say What You Are Doing button, 103

scheduling events, 13, 200, 203
    creating, 200-202
    sending invitations, 202

scrolling through videos, 139

Search box (toolbar), 11

searching
    classmates, 38
    companies/public figures, 173-177
    email contacts, 39
    games, 208-209
    groups, 182-183

security
    Check In feature (iPhone), 19
    locations, adding to posts, 101
    passwords, 6

sending text messages, 159-165

settings (accounts), configuring, 227-228

Settings (gear) button, 9

sharing
    buttons, 107
    photos, 144-152, 222, 250
    posts, 93, 124-127, 219-220
    status updates, 74-75, 219-220
    on updates, 67-68
    videos, 141, 144-152, 222
    website content, 107-108
    YouTube videos, 154-155

shorthand (abbreviations), writing posts/status updates, 118-120

sidebar menus, 10
  left side menu, 12
  News Feed, 69
  right side menu, 14
signing into/out of accounts, 8-9
signing up for Facebook, 4-7
  email
    addresses, 6
    confirmation, 7
  passwords, 6
  security, 6
single-player games, 207
slideshow video of photos, 156
smartphones
  Android, 26-29
  iPhone, 18-21
  Messenger app, 163-168
social games
  player, 207
  third-party games, 208
social networks, goal of, 4
spelling in posts/status updates, 118
starting video chats, 170
status updates, 4, 63
  abbreviations (shorthand) in, 118-120
  attention-seeking updates, 116
  bad updates, avoiding, 114-116
  commenting on, 67, 74
  complaining in, 115
  confessions in, 115
  defining, 95
  deleting, 57
  etiquette. See also manners
    abbreviations (shorthand), 118-120
    grammar, 118
    misspellings, 118
    writing updates, 117

family updates, etiquette and, 223-224
frequency of, determining, 121
friends, tagging, 102
good updates, writing, 111
  important information, 113-114
  interesting information, 112-113
grandchildren, 219-220, 223-224
hashtags (#), 97
hiding, 57
law enforcement, 115
liking, 66, 73
links, posting, 98
locations, posting, 100-101
meaningless updates, 116
mobile apps
  posting, 96
  viewing, 62-68
opinions in, 115
personal information in, 115-116
photos
  embarrassing photos in, 115
  posting, 99-100, 145
posting, 98, 103-108, 145
privacy, 104-106, 220-221
  confessions, 115
  personal information, 115-116
Publisher box, 97
sharing, 67-68, 74-75
tagging friends, 95
vague, 116
viewing, 63-64, 70-72, 258
websites, viewing, 68-75
streaming live video, 156
surveys, 86-87

T

tablets, iPads, 22-24

tagging, 96
  friends
    in photos, 150
    in status updates, 102, 142
  managing, 129-130
  yourself in friends photos, 142

Tag People in Your Post button, 102, 188

Tag Photo button, 142

text chats
  grandchildren, 222
  Messenger app, 163-168

text messages
  reading, 161
  sending, 159-165
  viewing, 162

third-party games, 208

Timeline, 45
  Activity Log, 58
  cover images, 52-54
  customizing, 47, 50-53
  editing, 54-55, 58
  privacy, 55-56, 133
  profile pictures, 47
  profiles, 54-56
  updating, 54-55
  viewing, 12, 45-27

time slider control (video), 139

toolbar, 11
  Friend Requests button, 11
  Friends button, 36, 39
  Messages button, 11
  Notifications button, 11
  Search box, 11

Trending section, 14

trending topics, 92

Twitter, 4, 225

U

unfriending friends, 42-43

Universal Windows Platform. *See* UWP, 255

universities or colleges, finding friends
  from, 38

unliking pages, 179

untagging yourself from friends
  photos, 143

updates (status)
  abbreviations (shorthand) in, 118-120
  attention-seeking updates, 116
  bad updates, avoiding, 114-116
  commenting on, 74
  complaining in, 115
  confessions in, 115
  defining, 95
  etiquette. *See also* manners
    abbreviations (shorthand), 118-120
    grammar, 118
    misspellings, 118
    writing updates, 117
  family updates, etiquette and, 223-224
  frequency of, determining, 121
  friends, tagging, 102
  good updates, writing, 111
    important information, 113-114
    interesting information, 112-113
  grandchildren, 219-220, 223-224
  hashtags (#), 97
  law enforcement, 115
  liking, 66, 73

links, posting, 98

locations, posting, 100-101

meaningless updates, 116

opinions in, 115

personal information in, 115-116

photos

  embarrassing photos in, 115

  posting, 99-100, 145

posting, 98, 103-108

privacy, 104-106, 220-221

  confessions, 115

  personal information, 115-116

Publisher box, 97

sharing, 74

tagging friends, 95

vague, 116

videos, 72, 145

viewing, 63-64, 70-71

updating

profile information, 54-55

status, 4, 63

uploading

photos, 146-152

videos, 141, 144

URLs (Uniform Resource Locators), deleting, 98

UWP (Universal Windows Platform), 255

V

vague posts, avoiding, 116

videos. *See also* photos

albums, viewing, 141

chats, 168

  ending, 171

  grandchildren, 222

installing chat applet, 170

microphones, 171

webcams, 171

posting to status updates, 99-100

processing, 145

scrolling through, 139

slideshow of photos, 154

sharing, 144-152, 222

status updates, 145

time slider control, 139

uploading, 144

viewing, 65, 72, 137-139

volume, raising or lowering, 139

YouTube videos, sharing, 154-155

View Activity Log button, 58

viewing

Activity Log, 58

Event page, 197-199

Facebook Pages, 175-178

groups, photos, 190

Moments apps, 250

Most Recent Posts, 69-70

News Feeds, 62, 68-69

photos, 71, 136, 140

pictures, 64

posts, 176

status updates, 63, 70

  mobile apps, 62-68

  websites, 68-75

text messages, 162

Timelines, 45-47

today's birthdays, 204

updates, 258

videos, 65, 72, 137-139, 141

web page links, 64, 71

visiting group pages, 186-187

volume, raising or lowering in videos, 139

W

webcams and video chats, 171

weblinks, etiquette, 117

web pages
  linking, 88, 98
  viewing, 64, 71

websites
  BuzzFeed, 88
  content, sharing, 107-108
  cover images, adding, 53
  Facebook sharing buttons, 107
  friends
    accepting/declining requests, 42
    finding, 35-38
  games
    managing, 211-213
    playing, 210-211
    searching, 208-209
  pictures, changing, 50-51
  status updates
    posting, 97
    viewing, 68-75
  text messages
    reading, 161
    sending, 159-165
    viewing, 162
  Timelines, accessing, 47
  video chats, 170

What Are You Doing? box, 103

Where Are You? button, 100

Who Are You With? button, 102

widescreen displays, 14

Windows 10 app, 255-258

workplace, finding friends from, 38

Y

YouTube
  linking accounts to, 155
  sharing videos, 154-155
  viewing, 72

Z

Zuckerberg, Mark, 4

More Best-Selling **My** Books!

Learning to use your smartphone, tablet, camera, game, or software has never been easier with the full-color My Series. You'll find simple, step-by-step instructions from our team of experienced authors. The organized, task-based format allows you to quickly and easily find exactly what you want to achieve.

Visit quepublishing.com/mybooks to learn more.

REGISTER THIS PRODUCT
SAVE 35%*
ON YOUR NEXT PURCHASE!

⌨ How to Register Your Product

- Go to quepublishing.com/register
- Sign in or create an account
- Enter the 10- or 13-digit ISBN that appears on the back cover of your book or on the copyright page of your eBook

🔓 Benefits of Registering

- Ability to download product updates
- Access to bonus chapters and workshop files
- A 35% coupon to be used on your next purchase – valid for 30 days
  To obtain your coupon, click on "Manage Codes" in the right column of your Account page
- Receive special offers on new editions and related Que products

Please note that the benefits for registering may vary by product. Benefits will be listed on your Account page under Registered Products.

We value and respect your privacy. Your email address will not be sold to any third party company.

* 35% discount code presented after product registration is valid on most print books, eBooks, and full-course videos sold on QuePublishing.com. Discount may not be combined with any other offer and is not redeemable for cash. Discount code expires after 30 days from the time of product registration. Offer subject to change.

quepublishing.com